Blessed

as a

Survivor

Memories of a Childhood in War and Peace

Elizabeth M. Wilms

Inspiring Voices®
A Service of **Guideposts**

B   (N)
WILMS
WIL
(124)

Inspiring Voices books may be ordered through booksellers or by contacting:

Inspiring Voices
1663 Liberty Drive
Bloomington, IN 47403
www.inspiringvoices.com
1-(866) 697-5313

ISBN: 978-1-4624-0711-8 (sc)
ISBN: 978-1-4624-0712-5 (e)

Library of Congress Control Number: 2013914677

Printed in the United States of America.

Inspiring Voices rev. date: 8/22/2013

To my sons, Friedrich and Michael, and my
grandchildren, Mina and Peter.

Be strong and courageous. Do not be terrified;
do not be discouraged, for the Lord, your God,
will be with you wherever you go.

—Joshua 1:9 (*Today's Light Bible,* New International
Version, Concordia Publishing House, 1999)

Table of Contents

Illustrations

Foreword

Over the past five decades, many of us have immersed ourselves in reading, researching, writing, and speaking about the history and experience of the Danube Swabians (Donauschwaben) before and after World War II. We welcome Elizabeth Wilms and her memoir to the ever-growing body of literature now available.

Those of us with roots in the villages and towns of the Danube basin searched desperately for news of our cousins overseas, in many cases while we were in Canadian or American army and navy uniforms. Upon our discharge from the armed forces, we struggled to find any newspaper article or books on (what we later found out) the genocide in our former homelands.

The first writing I found was a 1947 book by Victor Gollanz. As a Jewish citizen of Britain and prominent publisher, he visited Germany to observe and report on the state of the broken country and its surviving residents. It was in his book that I first discovered the term "expellees" and along with it his courageous (and what proved to be a very wise) demand: "Abandon Potsdam."[1]

Then we had a clue: at the Potsdam Conference in the summer of 1945, the Allied leaders sanctioned the expulsion of German-speaking minorities in central and eastern Europe. Although it was to be a "humane and orderly" transfer of people, it turned into barbaric chaos.[2]

The consensus today is that fifteen million ethnic Germans were on the roads from deep inside Russia through eastern and northern Europe, in the bitter winter of 1944-45. They were part of the flight and then expulsion, and they were hopeful they would find a country that would give them refuge. Two million died en route. These figures have changed over the years from seventeen million, quoted by former President George Bush,[3] to fifteen million by former Chancellor Konrad Adenauer. Among the two million who died were unknown thousands of Danube Germans. Shocking but true: this was the largest forced migration of civilians in history.[4]

The term "Donauschwaben" (Danube Swabians) was not heard in the United States and Canada until the mid 1950s, when expellees of the Danube Basin emigrated to North America and formed numerous cultural Societies. (Thousands also live in Australia, Brazil, France, Austria, and Switzerland.)

The term was coined in a geography class in 1922, in Graz, Austria, by Professor Robert Sieger, to differentiate the Swabians of the Transdanubian countries (Hungary, Rumania, Yugoslavia) from the citizens of the state of Swabia in southern Germany. There has been some controversy as to whether it was Sieger or his student Herman Rudiger who originated this name for an ethnic group, because the first settlers originated in Swabia.[5]

This controversy seems unnecessary, as both the teacher and the student get credit for the term, which has attained scholarly acceptance. As long as the survivors and their children are alive, the Societies will remain active and the word may become well known. However, in another generation, it may disappear. For one thing, many still refer to themselves as German-Hungarian or Austro-Hungarians. When filling out census documents, the words "Danube Swabian" will be ignored, and most have learned to fill in the blank with the term "Germanic."

As for the present time, most of their Societies (Vereine) are proactive and welcomed in their communities for their monthly meetings, picnics, dances, choirs, student exchanges with their kin in Europe, weekend language schools, and their work toward building museums or archive centers filled with the literature, art, recordings, and film chronicling their history and experience.

Lake Villa, near Chicago, is a good example. Outdoor and indoor activities are held year round, and here is where they have erected a beautiful monument to those who did not survive. A yearly Mass is held to honor and remember those who died in the camps. Young people join the parade, holding crosses with the names of many of the extermination camps—a very touching scene for all who gather there. Local and state politicians and clergy are always invited and can see how devastated these people are with the loss of their homelands.

Another little known and sad chapter in the history of the Yugoslavian Swabians is the separation of parents from their children. Statistics are often unreliable, but one figure states that between thirty-five and forty thousand children under the age of sixteen were separated from their parents.[6] Many were taken to state orphanages and kept there to be indoctrinated by communist teachers. After the war, the International Red Cross tried valiantly to reunite these children with parents or surviving relatives. During an interview with some of these children, now adults, I learned that there were a few traveling Catholic nuns who visited these orphanages (*Kinderheime*). While there, they tried to make up little poems for each of the children so they would remember their names when parents came to find them. After some years, the children would forget, especially the younger ones. Some remembered, and reconciliation occurred.

I can never forget one poem recited during our conversation:
"My name is Michael Schneider
I come from Apatin.
My mother is Susanna
My father, Valentin."

While many returned to their families, some chose to stay with the Serbian parents who had taken them in. One can only imagine the pain of the rejected parents.

At a Milwaukee Donauschwaben picnic in 1970, I noted a mother and daughter happily dancing together. I asked one of the women at my table who they were. She looked shocked at my request but hesitantly she told me the story. Suffice it to say, they were not mother and daughter. But the mother had been searching for years for her little girl, a mere infant when she was taken away. It was not until 1950, after most orphanages had been emptied, that she found this little five-year-old, who was as yet unclaimed, sitting quietly in a corner of the almost-abandoned building. Since she could not find her own child, she told the director she was sure this was her "Lissi." To this day, I do not know if she ever told the girl that she was not really her biological child.

There may have been many stories like this. One can only hope that all the lost children found homes.

Thanks to the American Aid Society in Chicago, there was a treasure trove of archival materials going back many decades, to a time when earlier Swabian immigrants arrived in the United States. Over many years they published several volumes titled *American Aid Societies Bulletin: For the Needy and Displaced Persons of Central and Southeastern Europe*. These carefully preserved bulletins allowed Professor Raymond Lohne to immerse himself into this material and led him to meet and interview many current members of the Society. He discovered that two of their members were instrumental in lobbying the US Congress to pass an immigration bill for the refugees and displaced persons of World War II, even those who were displaced ethnic Germans, allowing them entry into the United States. Two leaders were Nick Pesch and John Meiszner. They succeeded in bringing almost fifty-four thousand Danube Swabians to the United States.[7]

In recent years, many scholars have realized that time is running out and survivors are now at an age when they are ready "to speak for the silent." A documentation project committee was formed to work on a definitive study of the wartime and postwar internments and atrocities to determine as accurately as possible how many people died in the camps (these were no camps as such, but rather, the actual villages and towns of the Swabians were surrounded by barbed wire and partisan guards).

The book *Genocide of Ethnic Germans in Yugoslavia 1944-48* is the result of many years of painstaking research and lists more than eighty of these camps by name, with the numbers of deaths in each. There is an English edition in addition to a German one.[8] Certainly, graduate students and those writing doctoral theses will find this invaluable. There seems to be a resurgence of interest in this topic, as you will see if you surf the Internet.

The April/May 2013 issue of *German Life* contains an interview with Professor Ali Botein-Furrevig, a professor of English at Ocean County College, New Jersey. She is also a director at the college's Center for Peace, Genocide, and Holocaust Studies. She states that there is a "disturbing veil of silence surrounding the bloody carnage unleashed by Tito against the Danube Swabians during the postwar years." Botein-Furrevig's latest book, *Last Waltz on the Danube,*[9] is her successful effort at lifting this "veil" in a truly humanitarian but objective manner.

Another successful effort to lift that veil of silence, and indeed to set aside a taboo that has lasted too many years, is *Blessed as a Survivor: Memories of a Childhood in War and Peace,* the biography ("lived history") of Elizabeth Wilms. This book is written from a different perspective than many earlier publications. Rather than convey crimes and brutality in a graphic manner—in other words, to speak the unspeakable and print the unprintable—this author prefers a matter-of-fact, guarded style of communicating. Those readers interested in painful narratives can find them in the literature readily available. As for the undercurrent of family dynamics in the author's work, one can only say: If the truth can set you free, perhaps the "telling" can heal the heart.

Eve Eckert Koehler, Author
Freelance Writer/Editor
Canadian Navy Veteran
Genealogy Researcher
June 2013

References

1   Gollancz, Victor. *In Darkest Germany: The Record of a Visit.* Illinois: Henry Regnery Co., 1947.

2   de Zayas, Alfred M. *Nemesis at Potsdam.* London: Routledge Kegan Paul, 1977.

3   de Zayas, Alfred M. *A Terrible Revenge.* Translation by John A. Koehler. See Foreword by Professor Charles Barber. New York: St. Martin's Press, Palgrave/Macmillan1994. Also Vardy, Steven and Hunt Tooley, eds. *Ethnic Cleansing in Twentieth Century Europe.* Foreword by Otto von Habsburg. New York: Columbia University Press, 2003.

4   de Zayas, Alfred. *Fifty Theses on the Expulsion of the Germans from Central and Eastern Europe 1944-48.* London: Inspiration Unlimited, 2012.

5   Scherer, Anton. *50 Jahre Stammesname.* Vierteljahresblatter: Donauschwaben & Sudostdeutsche, 1994. Also Stenger Frey, Katherine. *The Danube Swabians. A People with Portable Roots.* Belleville Ontario: Mika Publishing Co., 1982.

6   Paikert, Geza. *The Danube Swabians.* The Hague: Martinus Nijhoff, 1967. Also Springenschmid, Karl. *Our Lost Children: Janissaries?* Translation by John A. Koehler, Published by the Danube Swabian Association, USA. Milwaukee WI: Schmidt Bros. Printer, 1981.

7   Lohne, Raymond. *The Great Chicago Refugee Rescue.* Rockport, ME: Picton Press, 1997.

8   Prokle, Herbert, George Wildmann, et al. *Genocide of the Ethnic Germans in Yugoslavia 1944-48.* Munich: Donauschwaben Kultur Stiftung, 2006.

9   Botein-Furrevig, Ali. *Last Waltz on the Danube: The Ethnic German Genocide in History and Memory.* Margate: ComteQ Publishing, 2012.

Acknowledgments

This book is a loving tribute to those many thousands who did not survive.

I want to thank my family and all my friends for their eager support and encouragement to write my life story.

The cover design was inspired by my granddaughter, Mina Wilms. A heartfelt thank you, Mina, for your important contribution to my story.

To Annerose Goerge, Danube Swabian Association of the United States, my sincere thanks for providing the book *Genocide of the Ethnic Germans in Yugoslavia 1944-48* and her generous permission to reprint the maps and any other material from the book.

I am exceptionally grateful to Mrs. Eve Eckert Koehler, who dedicated her life to the history of the Danube Swabians and authored the book *Seven Susannahs: Daughters of the Danube*. I do appreciate her encouraging words and her supporting material, especially for writing the foreword for my book. A well-deserved, hearty thank-you.

My thanks to Anita Pare, who made me aware of the information on the Internet about Molidorf.

Most of all, I would like to thank a member of my church congregation who does not want to be named, whose technical computer knowledge enabled me to complete this book. Without his help and support, this story would have never been published.

Introduction

In 1955, my parents, Nikolaus and Elisabeth Marx, my brother, Anton (Toni), and I immigrated from Germany to the United States. In this great country, we did not dwell on the unpleasant past with its unimaginable turmoil, since a new life full of hope and opportunities lay ahead of us. Our plight, as displaced ethnic Germans who had been separated and experienced many hardships, did not receive much public sympathy either. The atrocities of Nazi Germany were well known, and if there were reprisals against the German population at large, they were just "getting what they deserved."

I always knew my early childhood had been different and unusual and that my story should be told. But I had other priorities during my adult life. It was not until the 1990s that my experiences were brought back to the foreground. During this time, the former Yugoslavia was breaking apart, and the majority, the Serbian people, committed many brutalities against the minorities. This news motivated me to write my experiences since I had been one of their victims many years ago, after World War II.

I then tucked this short draft away into the closet with the idea that "one day I will write a book." But I never had the courage to tackle the undertaking, until I received a general e-mail from *Guideposts* that read, "Publish Your Book." I have been a subscriber to *Guidepost* magazine for many years, and I was familiar with their impeccable reputation. Without thinking about it, I answered the mailing of Inspiring Voices, a division of Guideposts.

Reopening the wounds of the past brought back many horrors from my childhood. I would wake up during the night, drenched in sweat, screaming for my husband, Fritz, or my mother. Reliving my life day and night was overwhelming. I could not continue this way. Like always, when there was trouble in my life, I started to pray, asking God to spare me from the nightmares. Yes, God did answer my prayers. My terrible dreams stopped.

Another thought that kept me going over the many months I worked on my memoir was a quote from Johann Wolfgang von Goethe: "Begin the web—God will supply the thread."

In this book I also describe my parents' World War II and postwar experiences. However, neither wished to go into detail about their past. I know more about my mother's life thanks to her second cousin, Anna Kuechel—I called her "Tante Anusch"—who recorded her life in German. She asked me to translate her thirty-two-page paper into English and gave me permission to use the information in my book. Tante Anusch and my mother spent their time as slave laborers in the Ukraine, Soviet Union, and had similar experiences. My father told me only one story from his war experience and a few highlights as a prisoner of war.

The names of the locations in my book have changed to the present language of the respective countries. I prefer to use the German names as I knew them for the villages and cities in my book.

The Banat region is a geographical and historical region in Central Europe. Currently it is divided between three countries: the eastern part lies in western Romania, the western part is in northwest Serbia, and a small northern part is in southeastern Hungary. We lived in the northwestern part, which was Yugoslavia but now belongs to the state of Serbia.

You may be wondering, *Why did your family as ethnic Germans live in the former Yugoslavia?* To answer this, I have to tell you the story of my ancestors, who settled in this part of Europe some two hundred years ago.

CHAPTER 1

The Journey of the Danube Swabians, 1692-1787

It was during the eighteenth century that many rulers extended a call to German settlers to relocate to their countries. In Prussia, Frederick the Great, and in Russia, Catherine the Great, who was a German princess, invited immigrants to resettle within their respective countries. In 1771 alone, twenty-six thousand Swabians from the southern part of Germany settled in the Ukraine, Russia, and Volga regions. Europe's longest river, the Volga, is some 2,290 miles long. The Transylvanian Saxons founded Hermannstadt and Kronstadt in the 1200s in what later became Romania. This area also was the home of the legendary Count Dracula. Even some rich Hungarian landowners extended invitations to settlers.

But of all the requests for immigration, the ruling Austrian Hapsburg offer was the most generous. The only requirement was that you had to be Catholic because the Hapsburgs defended their faith. Later on, however, exceptions were made, and even Protestants were allowed to immigrate.

There would be no taxes for three years. The farmland, animals, and equipment would all be free. It was simply too good to be true! The feudal system was still very much alive, and only a few landowners existed. So the Hapsburgs had to make a generous offer to ensure that a large group of settlers would come.

To begin with, streets, bridges, and postal stops had to be established. River traffic on the Danube and its major arteries was encouraged. Cities with German laws and customs were founded by attracting army veterans, craftsmen, and merchants from Germany and Austria. In addition to a certain desire for freedom, the settlers were lured by economic and social reasons. It is important to understand that people in those days seldom left the area of their birth, let alone their country. Immigrants also had to consider the uncertainties: separation from family and home, a different climate, many hardships in the wilderness, and illnesses such as malaria and typhoid fever. But even the many negative possibilities did not discourage settlers.

Usually, new communities were created on land owned by the crown. Nearly one thousand German farming communities were established in the Danube basin. It was only through the settling of farmers and numerous craftsmen in larger agrarian communities that the true recovery of the Danube region become definite and lasting. Through hard work, they transformed the wilderness, the swamps, and the steppes (prairies) by controlling the rivers and building canals. Other ethnic groups involved in this undertaking were Hungarians, Slavs, and Romanians.

As the immigrants received all these benefits, there were also obligations to be honored. For instance, no one could leave unless he or she repaid the government its expenses. If one left for any reason, including homesickness, that person was considered a fugitive from the law.

The Danube is the second-longest river in Europe, at 1,770 miles. It originates in the Black Forest in Swabia, a state in southern Germany, and flows through Austria, Hungary, Yugoslavia, Romania, and Bulgaria into the Black Sea. For transportation, some settlers used covered wagons and followed the roads along the Danube. Others took box boats going down the river. The city of Ulm in Germany was where many migrants boarded the box boats, *Ulmer Schachtel,* for the journey to their new home. The settlers stopped in Vienna, where they registered for their land.

The Danube Swabian settlements were located on both banks of the central Danube River—from the Raab River in the northwest to the Iron Gate in the southeast—within the dual monarchy Austria-Hungary. It has also been said that the area comprised the Balkan Peninsula, which is located in southeast Europe, between the Adriatic and Black seas. The Turks had left the area decimated and depopulated after 150 years of Ottoman rule. In 1692, the Turks were defeated at the gates of Vienna, and they retreated to south of Belgrade. By 1719, it was possible to get an imperial free pass to homestead in the Banat region.

During the eighteenth century, there were three larger Swabian migrations. The first migration, under Emperor Charles VI, happened between 1718 and 1737. Empress Maria Theresa sponsored the second migration from 1744-72. It was during this period that my ancestors settled in the three sister villages of St. Hubert, Charleville, and Soltur, in the area called Banat. The third and last migration occurred from 1782-87 under Emperor Joseph II.

Even though the settlers came from the southwest German states and spoke various dialects, they were called Danube Swabians, or *Donauschwaben.*

The hardships endured by the three groups is summarized in this stanza from a poem composed by unknown German settlers, found in the book *The Danube Swabians: A People with Portable Roots:*

"Der Erste hat den Tod,
Der Zweite hat die Not
Der Dritte erst hat Brot."
("The first encounters death,
The second need,
But only the third has bread.")

3

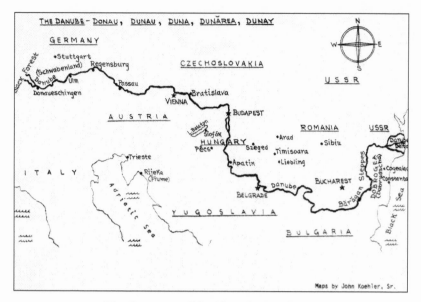

The Journey of the Danube Swabians
Map by John Koehler Sr.

CHAPTER 2

My Ancestors' Settlement in Soltur, 1772-1884

According to old documents from the three-sister-village book *Heimatbuch der Banater Schwestergemeinden: St. Hubert-Charleville-Soltur*, when my ancestors arrived in the area, the Austrian government offered each homesteader one Joch (equal to 1.4 acres) of land to build a home. The land the farmers received depended on the size of the family. Each farmer also had a share of three Joch on the commonly owned open space called *Hutweide*. A field of one Joch was set aside to grow hemp. The tough fibers of the plant were used to make ropes (to tie the harvest) and sailcloth. All total, they could receive thirty-five Joch of land, including the house lot, which is about forty-nine acres.

The method of farming they used was called the "open field system." Each year the treatment of the fields shifted in steady rotation so that each field lay fallow once every three years. This system was necessary at a time when methods of fertilizing were crude and unscientific. This kind of cultivation was almost universal throughout Europe. Each farmer also received a team of horses, farm equipment, a wagon, a cow, a pig, chickens, wheat enough for one year, seeds to plant the crops, furniture for one bedroom, and a kitchen set. For daily living expenses, each person in the family received two Kreuzer (pennies) until the family could support itself.

At first, the fields around the village were used to grow hemp. In later years, the fields were converted into vineyards. Grapes were used for eating as well as for winemaking. The specialty crops grown in the area were sugar beets and hemp. Other crops were wheat, corn, sunflowers, and alfalfa. Besides the grapes, we had peaches, apricots, melons, and tomatoes. The farmers also raised horses, cattle, pigs, chickens, and geese. Each household had a huge vegetable garden and grew flowers for decoration.

The Austrian government assistance program was not limited to farmers. Homesteading craftsmen also received assistance in the form of fifty Gulden cash to buy their tools. They were also entitled to the furniture, the wheat for one year, and the animals, except the horses.

The Danube Swabian communities exhibited the characteristics of organization and neatness, which definitely distinguished them from their multiethnic surroundings of the Serbs, Croats, and Hungarians.

The villages were planned with wide streets, a church in the center, city hall, a school, and a tavern, all were built close together at the central square. More space was calculated into the village design for markets, festivals, and sport fields. The plan included a cemetery, ponds for runoff water, a common grazing area, a hemp mill, a brickworks factory, and a blacksmith. Usually these newly created villages were self-contained farming communities or self-sufficient units. Most of the Danube Swabians living in small villages scattered throughout Yugoslavia, Hungary, and Romania were isolated from the rest of the Western world, including our three sister villages. Our language, customs, and culture had been handed down from generation to generation for hundreds of years.

Each village had at least one artesian well in the center. This well was drilled deep enough to reach water that was draining down from higher surrounding ground above the well so that the pressure forced a continuous upward flow of water. The water tasted great. The people carried the water home in large buckets to be used for drinking and cooking only. Each house had its own well for doing laundry, washing dishes, and watering the garden and farm animals.

The three sister villages were located on flat, low land, only about eighty meters, or seventy-three feet, above sea level. The villages were surrounded by ponds for the runoff rainwater.

Each village had its own grammar school. Several grades, from kindergarten to sixth, were combined in one room. After age twelve, no other schooling was required. Many young people became an apprentice in a trade, while others helped with the farming. Only a few people went on to higher learning in a big city. Within the family the people spoke the Swabian dialect, which is part of the German language. In school they were taught High German, the official spoken and written language of Germany.

St. Hubert, the largest of the three villages, had the honor of housing the Catholic church, which served all the people in the sister villages. St. Hubert also had a train station. The railroad may have reached us about one hundred years ago.

Our ancestors worked hard and were thrifty people. They also had wise hereditary practices. Only the eldest son would inherit the land, while the rest of the children had to find other livelihoods. Some went to the city to earn money; others went to Germany to learn a trade. When they returned, they opened up a shop. Later, many immigrated to foreign soil, like the United States, Canada, South America, and even Australia. The exit from the area was due to large families, who could not be supported by fewer than fifty acres, and there was no other industry in the area in which to earn a living.

Many of the first settlers died from intermittent raids by the Turks or by various plagues, such as the flooding of the Danube River, as well as other contributory rivers and canals in the area. While the rich black soil in the Banat region could produce an abundant harvest, it also was prone to huge floods. When this happened, the people lost their livelihood for the year. Without government assistance, some settlers accumulated great debts. There were years of drought and even earthquakes that damaged homes and added expenses. Sicknesses, such as malaria and typhoid fever, were very common, leaving the surviving spouse to support his or her big family alone.

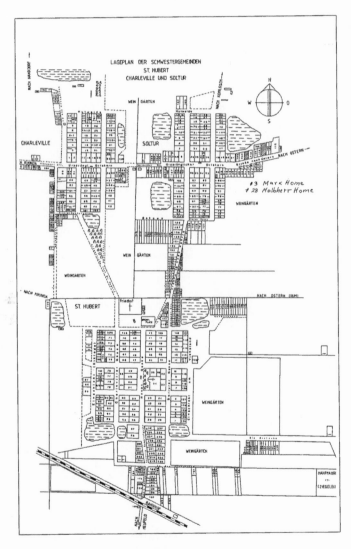

Site Plan of the Sister Villages—St. Hubert-Charleville-Soltur. Now It Is Called Banatsko Velico Selo

CHAPTER 3

A Wedding and a Honeymoon in Chicago, 1884-1925

My four grandparents were born in Soltur, Banat, in the Empire of Austria–Hungary. My father's ancestors came from the Black Forest area in Swabia, southern Germany. The family name is Marx. They first settled in Nakodorf and later moved to Soltur.

Anton Marx, born in 1884, and Magdalena Zachary, born in 1886, were my paternal grandparents. I called them Ota and Oma. They had four children: Christopher, born in 1908; Caroline, born in 1909; my father, Nikolaus, born in 1912; and Franz, born in 1921.

In 1906, my Marx grandparents came to Chicago, Illinois, to get married, since both sides of the family objected to their union. My Marx Oma came from a large family of nineteen children, but only five reached adulthood. My Marx Ota was a master carpenter and cabinetmaker and easily found work in Chicago. Here in this city, their first two children were born. My aunt, Caroline, was a sickly child. The doctor told my grandparents that the city's air pollution was not good for the infant.

In 1911, my Marx grandparents returned to Soltur. There my father was born, as well as his younger brother, Franz. Their assigned house number and mailing address was house number three.

In 1925, Uncle Chris and Aunt Caroline returned to the city of their birth, Chicago. Living here, Peter Zachary, a brother of my Marx Oma would look after the two young people. The plan was to stay only for a few years and then return to Soltur, but they remained in Chicago and never returned home.

Since my early years were mainly spent with my maternal grandparents, I have very few memories of my Marx Ota. But my Marx Oma became a big part of my life in later years. I always thought she was a tall woman, perhaps five feet, seven inches, with hazel eyes that could shimmer into the color green. She never had her hair cut during my childhood and wore her long hair gathered in a bun on top of her head. She became a widow in 1942 at age fifty-six and was completely dependent on my father for additional income when he took over Ota's carpenter shop after his father's death.

My mother's ancestors originated from Alsace-Lorraine, which is located west of the Rhine River and at the time was part of the Holy Roman Empire of the German Nations. Empress Maria Theresa's husband was Francis of Lorraine. He was elected emperor of the Holy Roman Empire. My mother's maiden name is Halbherr.

Lorenz Halbherr, born in 1884, and Anna Heidenfelder, born in 1895, had two children, Johann (Hans), born in 1912, and my mother, Elisabeth, named after her grandmother, born in 1915. My Halbherr Oma gave her children German names but called them by Hungarian nicknames. Johann became "Jani" and Elisabeth was known as "Erschi."

In January 1911, after my Halbherr grandparents were married, they decided on a long honeymoon trip to Chicago, Illinois. Oma worked as a seamstress at Hart/Schaffner and Marx, while Ota was a custodian in a factory. They saved every penny they could, even walking both ways to and from work to save the nickel bus ride. In 1912 they returned to Soltur. Oma was expecting her first child, Johann, and wanted to be with her mother when the baby arrived.

My Halbherr Ota, who was one of ten children, of which only three reached adulthood, was a merchant. He owned and operated a general store. He also was active in village government. An outgoing and friendly person, he was well-suited for the job. His house was conveniently located right next to the village hall, in the center of the village, having been assigned house number twenty-eight.

Ota, at around five feet, ten inches, appeared to be so much taller than Oma, who was only five feet tall. But his most striking characteristic was his eyes. They were sky-blue and always friendly. He was also very proud of his wine cellar, since it was customary in the area to drink wine with the noon dinner and evening supper. But Oma was always quick to point out that she "never saw her husband intoxicated."

Ota also was a kindhearted person, helping people wherever he could. With his trusting nature, he made many friends. His most precious possessions besides his family was his land. In his mind, land did not become worthless, like money could and did. Since he was such an easygoing person, he left the running of his household entirely up to Oma.

I heard about his courting method and how, at age twenty-seven, he finally found the woman he desired in my hardworking Oma, who was only sixteen. She did not disappoint him, even during World War I, when Ota was away at war serving as a medical corpsman.

She gladly told me about this difficult time in her life, full of responsibilities and hard work. She had two young children, her son, only two years old, and my mother, born in 1915. Every day she would rise at four a.m. to feed the animals. She had to milk the cow, feed the pigs (which were raised for additional income), and feed the chickens. If she decided on a chicken dinner for the day, she had to catch it first before letting the rest out into the yard. Monday was laundry day, a time-consuming project. Another day of the week was designated for baking bread and other pastries. Her mother-in-law helped by looking after the children, but she also managed the general store. Each day she took care of the house, when needed worked in the vegetable garden, and tended the vineyards. She always closed with this statement: "I did it willingly and never complained."

Oma's remark was mainly meant for my mother, who usually was close by listening in and had a poor attitude toward her caretaking responsibilities. My mother performed her daily chores reluctantly and with open resentment.

CHAPTER 4

World War I, 1914-18, The Treaty of Trianon, 1920

Big changes were about to happen in our part of the world with the outbreak of World War I.

In 1914 a Serbian assassin in Sarajevo shot and killed Archduke Francis Ferdinand of Austria/Hungary. His wife, who was with him, was also killed. Austria demanded that the assassin be delivered to them, but Serbia refused.

This triggered World War I in 1914.

The Central Powers were Germany, Austria/Hungary, Turkey, and Bulgaria. The opposition during the war were the "Big Four"—Great Britain, France, Italy, and the United States. The Central Powers also fought against Russia, but due to its 1917 revolution, Russia formally withdrew and signed its own peace treaty with Germany.

World War I ended on November 11, 1918. Our area suffered no war damages, since all actions took place north of the Banat.

In 1919, the Treaty of Versailles was signed under protest by Germany, since it demanded a sum of thirty-three billion dollars for war reparation, besides the loss of territory and population.

In the "Treaty of Trianon" in June 1920, the Austrian/Hungarian Empire was carved up and new countries were created. Austria was separated from Hungary, and Czechoslovakia, Yugoslavia, and Romania were formed. Galicia was given to Poland. Hungary had lost two-thirds of its territory and one-half of its population. The Banat region, with its ethnic group of Danube Swabians, was divided against its will into the three successor states of the Danube Monarchy: Yugoslavia, Romania, and Hungary, making them a distinct "minority" in each state. Our area was given to Yugoslavia, with Belgrade serving as its capital city and the Serbs in control of the government. One consequence of this was the devaluation of our currency from Gulden to dinar. The official language was Serbian, and the official head of the state was a Serbian king. More than five hundred thousand Danube Swabians who lived in the area became a minority, and thus we were ruled by the majority.

Under the Serbian rule, restrictions were placed on the Danube Swabians; for example, the people could no longer acquire real estate. Other southeastern people in the region were Hungarians, Romanians, Serbs, Croats, and Slovenians. The latter three groups share the same ethnic roots but were divided because of their religious beliefs: some were Roman Catholics, others were part of the Greek Orthodox Church, and the third group belonged to the Islam faith. The religious conflict among these groups was one reason that contributed to the final breakup of Yugoslavia many years later.

In our agrarian culture, where the primary mode of transportation was a horse and buggy, not much changed. Our three villages remained almost untouched. We still spoke our Swabian dialect and learned High German in school. We had a German priest and continued our customs and festivals like before. However, a person seeking a higher education was required to master the Serbian language.

The Dissolution of Austria-Hungary.
The heavy dotted line bounds the old Austrian-Hungarian
Monarchy. The light dotted lines show the several provinces.
The heavy solid lines bound the new states formed by the Paris
Conference as follows: 1. The Republic of Austria; 2. The
Republic of Hungary; 3. The Republic of Czechoslovakia;
4. Austrian territories annexed to Poland; 5. Hungarian
territories annexed by Rumania; 6. The Serbo-Croat-Slovene
State Yugoslavia; 7. Austrian territory annexed by Italy

CHAPTER 5

My Birth in Hettin, Yugoslavia, 1938-39

My parents, Nikolaus Marx, a cabinetmaker, and Elisabeth Halbherr, a homemaker, were married at St. Hubert's Catholic church on November 9, 1933. Both were born in Soltur, Banat, Austria/Hungary. They attended the same school and knew each other all their lives.

Both were of average height, my father five feet, eight inches and my mother about five feet, four inches. While my mother's eyes were brown, my father had hazel eyes, which at times appeared green. Since housing was limited, they lived with either of their parents until my father was hired as the local band director by the village of Hettin, about ten miles southeast of Soltur. He also gave private music lessons to students. His favorite musical instrument was the violin, but he also played the accordion and the tuba.

I was born on January 16, 1938, their firstborn, during my parents' stay in Hettin. I was named after my mother and Marx Oma: Elizabeth Magdalena, nicknamed "Lisl." At the time it was customary to have children immediately after marriage. So later on I wondered why they waited for more than four years to have me. My father, whom I called "Tata," never discussed anything intimate about his life with me. So I asked my mother, whom I called

"Mama." Her answer to me was "Your father always said that he did not want to be a young grandfather," so they waited. I had my doubts about this explanation.

After I was born, each one of my grandmothers came to help out for a week. They took the fastest mode of travel during the middle of the winter, a horse-drawn sleigh ride over the snow-covered and icy roads. Children were born at home, with a midwife in attendance. Women were required to stay in bed much longer and recovery was slower, compared to what is practiced today.

When I look at my early baby pictures, I see a chubby infant with blonde hair, which a year later appeared all white. I also inherited my mama's brown eyes.

For as long as I can remember, Halbherr Oma would tell me her reaction when she first saw me. "This is going to be my granddaughter, who will take care of me when I am old and sick." To this day I cannot believe that I never challenged her. Why did she not expect her daughter, my mama, to take care of her? Was she not next in line?

I was taught to respect my elders, and therefore I did not question what they said. To confront them or challenge their wisdom was not acceptable. However, I did resent the fact that at my birth, Oma had chosen a role for my life of service to her.

Mama would tell me many times that I was a "naughty" child. I expected to be held and carried around, even when she did her chores. I also did not take any more naps after I was six months old. Mama would place me in my cradle, which Tata built, and rock it to get me to sleep. I doubt that she sang to me because I know she could not carry a tune. As soon as she thought I was asleep, and she stopped the rocking, my eyes opened, and I was wide awake. Years later, when she talked about it, she still became upset.

I believe that even as a young child, I sensed my mother's feelings toward me. As long as she rocked me, my caretaker was there. When the rocking stopped, I was on high alert. *Is she going to leave me?* My desire to be carried around and be held by her were proof of my need to be near her.

There is some evidence that the sense of belonging, of being loved and wanted, begins before birth, according to *Healing for Damaged Emotions* by David A. Seamands. I do believe my behavior as a baby reflected my feelings of insecurity. Of course a little nap on my part would have given Mama some relief. I can sympathize with that. Later I had the feeling that she wanted me to feel "guilty" for being such a difficult child. She also breastfed me up to one year. She told me I bit her nipples and made them sore. I never knew what to say about that. I was just a baby and did not know what I was doing.

Mama loved to tell this story, and I heard it countless times. She had an appointment and left Tata in charge of me. He, however, needed to concentrate on his work. He had to hand copy the musical scores for his students. I was about one year old and was fascinated with chicken eggs. We raised our own chickens for their eggs and eventual meat consumption. Tata had this great idea to keep me quiet. He sat me in the middle of the stone kitchen floor and placed a basket of fresh chicken eggs in front of me. As a result, he had his quiet time, and I had much fun cracking, squashing, and throwing eggs and sliding around in the mess. I can visualize myself sitting gleefully among the crushed eggs and having a wonderful time.

When Mama returned home and saw me, she became very upset. Now she had to clean me up, as well as the kitchen floor. I would have been unhappy too. Even many years later, she became as angry about it as she was on the day it happened. When I think about it now, I believe it must have been a hilarious scene. However, she never had a sense of humor, so even years later she was never able to laugh about it.

In defense of Tata, I must say that during the 1930s the roles and responsibilities of males and females were clearly defined. The man was the breadwinner and did most of the hard physical repair work around the house. Women were the nurturers and caretakers of the family and home. They did the cooking, cleaning, sewing, shopping, laundry, and child raising. Only for grave offenses, or when the children were older, did the father take over.

Tata believed in this kind of cultural tradition. This was the way he was raised, and that is what his father modeled for him. Mama, however, did not fully accept her responsibilities and she complained a lot, since she wanted Tata to help her.

Mama was a skilled seamstress. She made all the dresses and coats for the family as well as jackets and shirts for Tata. Since all household chores needed to be done from scratch, a woman's day was filled with taking care of the children, cooking, baking, cleaning the house, doing the laundry, feeding and watering the livestock, tending the vegetable garden, and canning the food for winter.

Everyone also helped out in the vineyard. The vines had to be pruned, tied to the poles, weeded, and sprayed. Then came the harvesting of the grapes and the winemaking.

Life was not easy. But at this time, most people had no idea what real hardships were. Soon we would find out, with the beginning of World War II.

CHAPTER 6

World War II, September 1939–May 1945

The Great Depression in Germany contributed to the decline of the moderates and the rise and triumph of Adolph Hitler's National Socialists.

Hitler was born in Austria, and he also fought during World War I. He felt the Treaty of Versailles after World War I was unfair to the German people. The Rhineland, the most industrialized area in Germany, had been occupied by the French for many years. Germany was unable to repay its war reparation to its former opponents. Hitler promised the German people that he would put everyone to work and that he wanted to regain the lost territories. He began building the Autobahn and also promised a Volkswagen for every family.

Hitler was elected by the German people. While in power, he became a dictator. Anyone who dared voice opposition or a critique against Hitler or the government was arrested and placed in prison or camps. A propaganda machine selected the news on radio or the newspaper regarding what the German people were told.

The Nazis felt the Jewish people were to blame for all the wrongs in Germany and indoctrinated the population accordingly. Millions of people died in concentration camps, including Jews, Poles, Czechs, Serbs, and even Germans who dared to speak up. It was a sad and terrible time.

In 1938 Adolph Hitler annexed Austria to Germany without any problem. Next, Czechoslovakia was absorbed into greater Germany with the pretense that it was not an annexation but only the incorporation of German-populated areas. Next, Hitler demanded a corridor from Poland, so Germany would be connected again to East Prussia. Poland refused. World War II began on September 1, 1939, when Hitler attacked Poland and conquered it in eighteen days. Then Hitler overran Denmark, Norway, the Netherlands, and Belgium. France capitulated after several weeks of fighting in 1940.

The Axis powers included Nazi Germany and Fascist Italy, with Japan joining in December 1941. Allies to Nazi Germany were Austria, Hungary, and Romania. Yugoslavia, with its Serbian king, Peter II, still had a good relationship with Hitler's Third Reich. By 1941, Italy, an ally with Germany, was fighting in Greece and needed help. Hitler asked if the German troops could move through Yugoslavia to get to Greece. A Serbian minister signed a pact in the "Wiener Vertrag" (Vienna Contract) to permit the request, but when he came home, he was arrested.

Coming from Romania, German planes bombed the capital city, Belgrade, on April 6, 1941. On April 11 and 12, German troops marched into Yugoslavia. Six days later, the Yugoslavian army surrendered. The king and its court had fled the country.

By 1942, the Yugoslavian communist party under its leader Marshall Tito (born Josip Broz, 1892-1980) was fighting the troops loyal to the Serbian king. Soon the communists also attacked the occupying German forces, which had been reduced in numbers. German troops had been pulled out of Yugoslavia for the invasion of the Soviet Union, which began in June of 1941.

The German army needed replacements. So in April 1942, all German men in Yugoslavia, Hungary, and Romania were drafted into the German army. Some 136,000 men from the southeast were forced to join the German military forces.

Men born between 1892 and 1924 were conscripted into the Seventh Mountain Division, called "Prinz Eugen", for the sole purpose of the defense of the Banat.

CHAPTER 7

Early Childhood Memories, 1942-44

The Seventh Mountain Division included my father and many men from our sister villages. Their mission was to keep peace in Yugoslavia and fight Marshall Tito's partisans. These men were an organized civilian force conducting guerilla warfare. After the war, Tito took over the country as a dictator and president in 1953. He had promised his troops the rich and fertile soil of the Danube Swabians as a reward.

In 1939 we returned to Soltur. Tata was needed in Ota's cabinetmaker shop. On weekends Tata still played in the local band for entertainment and extra income. Tata's younger brother, Franz, died in 1940 of tuberculosis at age nineteen. This was a very tragic event for our family.

My earliest memories go back to the spring of 1942, when I was just four years old. We lived with my Marx grandparents in the same house but with a private entrance to our three-room apartment. My grandfather Anton Marx died in early March 1942. I only recall his funeral and have no other memory of him. He was laid out on his bed with the entire room darkened with black curtains and wall hangings. There were no funeral homes, and the wake happened in the house of the deceased. I was carried into the room and asked to give my grandfather a kiss, which I did not want to do. The entire setting and the corpse sent shivers down my spine. But I was compelled to do it. To this day, I do not care to think about this unpleasant episode in my life.

In my next memory, Tata put me to bed after I said my prayers. This was most unusual, because Mama always put me to bed at night. I recall that I asked for my mama. Tata's answer escaped my memory, but I still see his face with tears in his eyes. This made a big impression on me because men never cried.

The following Sunday, Tata dressed me for church in my Sunday's best dress. He had a black armband on his coat, which indicated that the family was in mourning. We walked hand in hand down Main Street. When we arrived at the corner, we had to turn right to head for St. Hubert, where the church for the three sister villages was located. I saw my Halbherr Ota out on the street. He came toward us, shouting and shaking his fist. Tata was still holding my hand when I saw and heard my mother calling, "Lisl, my child, come to me." Tata let my hand go, and I ran into my mama's arms.

I had no idea what happened between my parents. All I knew was that Mama walked out on Tata and left me behind. I assume my grandparents did not agree with their daughter's actions. Ever-concerned about their image in a small village, this situation had to be corrected. After all, what loving mother would leave her child behind when she walks out on her husband?

Shortly thereafter, in late April 1942, my father was drafted into the German army. I have no memory of saying good-bye to Tata. Mama and I stayed with her parents. We never moved back into the apartment we shared as a family. During the summer of 1942, I was told to watch the common storks, who soon would be bringing me a baby brother or sister. I questioned this prediction. How could a stork come through the window and bring a baby? Of course I had all kind of questions. But Mama found my constant inquisitiveness annoying.

On Sunday, September 13, 1942, my brother, Anton, called Toni, was born and named after our Marx Ota. Toni also inherited both his grandfathers' blue eyes and blond hair. Yes, I was thrilled to have a little baby brother.

December 6 was St. Nikolaus Day. The night before I was asked to polish and shine my shoes and place them on the windowsill. During the night St. Nikolaus would stop by with sweet treats for well-behaved children. But naughty children would receive a switch and other undesirable things. The Christmas tree was brought all decorated on Christmas Eve by the "Christkindl" (Christ child). Usually a neighbor would be dressed up in an all white robe (bed sheets), with a white beard and a head-cover disguise. He also brought all the other presents. But first he asked me if I had been a good girl, and I had to recite my prayers. Christmas and birthday presents consisted mainly of needed clothes. I received very few toys, but I do remember two of my presents, my dolls, named Louise and Lydia. Tata had built me a wooden buggy for them, of which I have a picture.

I was around five years old when I became skeptical of this man and suspected I knew him. Having been an honest, straightforward little girl, I informed everyone about my doubts. During the summer, I discovered my mother's hiding place for the Christmas presents. I have to admit that I was a curious child and might have deliberately searched for evidence. Anyway, I gleefully confronted my mama about the discoveries and her deception toward me. I remember the confrontation happened on the porch, in front of the kitchen. Mama and Oma were present.

Mama became furious and lost all control. Mama told me I was going up into the dark attic stairway. Oma felt sorry for me and pleaded, "Don't do that to the child." But Mama responded angrily, "Nothing doing; I will show her." She dragged me screaming and crying to the dark attic entrance and locked me in.

Attics were huge, accessible by a wide stairway. These lofty attics also prevented a heat buildup during the summer. My grandparents' house was directly connected with a stable. The stairway provided access to the house attic and the stable lofts. The stable housed a cow for our milk, as well as several hundred chickens. This type of construction permitted rodents to enter in abundance. Mice loved the attics, and rats found their way into the stable and up into the lofts.

I knew this and was simply terrified of the rodents and the dark. I was screaming and pleading with my mother to let me out, promising I would never do it again. In my mind, I had done something terribly wrong; therefore, I had to show remorse. I have no idea how long she kept me locked up, but I remember the terror she created in me. To this day, I am petrified of a tiny mouse, to say nothing of the much larger rat. I do believe my mother overreacted with her punishment, but I never held this against her. I always felt she did what she knew was customary in our village. But still, in her heart, my mother loved me.

I also recall playing doctor with my girlfriend Heidi. My bed was located in the kitchen, around which we placed chairs and draped old sheets over them. We crawled under to play a game of pretend, as children do. Someone was still in the room, so he or she heard what was said, even though the person did not see everything we did to each other. As little girls do, we pretended to listen to our chest and tummy area. It was an innocent game. We imitated what the doctor did to us. The object I used to listen to my friend's heart was warm when my mother pulled the bed sheets away. She concluded that we had done improper things that required consequences.

Heidi was sent home. Mama placed dried corn kernels on the floor and made me kneel on them. I was instructed not to hunch back but to kneel straight up, so that my entire weight was resting on those hard kernels. This punishment hurt very much, especially since some time passed before I was allowed to get up.

Even this incident I never held against Mama, even though this time I had done nothing wrong. I knew my mother could not tolerate any kind of criticism. She seldom, if ever, admitted she had made a mistake. Many people had this mindset at the time: parents did not admit to have made a mistake because that weakened their authority, and therefore they would lose control. In other words, parents were always right.

In 1943, on my first day in Kindergarten, I threw a tantrum when Mama tried to leave without me. I guess I misread Mama that day, because normally she loved it when I clung to her. That particular day, I embarrassed her in front of other people. The dark attic stairway was my punishment for the second time.

When I look at my pictures from that period, I see a smiling girl with braids who had lost weight. This was caused by my frequent attacks of tonsillitis, which struck me throughout my entire childhood.

CHAPTER 8

The Sweet Scent of the Acacia Trees, Summer 1944

Tonsillitis was a major childhood illness for me, striking several times each year. The severe inflammation of my tonsils was accompanied by very high temperatures. Since my episodes happened before the age of penicillin, only home remedies were known to help me recover. If sponging down my body with rubbing alcohol and taking aspirin did not sufficiently reduce my fever, then Mama and Oma would take a sheet, soak it in cold water, wring it out, and wrap my entire body in it. To this day, when I remember how it felt, I shiver. For my sore throat, I was given honey-sweetened herbal teas, such as chamomile, peppermint, or linden tree blossom tea.

I recall visiting many doctors with Mama. Some told her, "Your daughter will outgrow this." Others recommended surgery. One doctor felt that my tonsils were small but deceased. This went on for at least two or three years, during which my tonsillitis became more frequent and severe.

After a particularly long period of wrestling with this illness and being confined to a dark room, I finally recovered. I still felt very weak from the high fever and the little nourishment I was able to take. Mama allowed me to sit outside in the warm sunshine in my little wicker chair. It was springtime, and nature had been reborn. I recall the sensations and overwhelming feelings I experienced that pleasant, warm day. I was so happy to be alive in the bright sunshine, surrounded by colorful flowers, trees, and bushes, all in full bloom. I will always remember the sweet scent of the many acacia trees, which gave me a feeling of contentment. I felt as if I had just emerged from a dark dungeon into a bright light of hope and peace. I was only six, but this beautiful feeling never left me. Throughout the years, I have revisited the comforting memories of contentment to help me deal with many hardships.

I have no idea what prompted Mama in the summer of 1944 to have my tonsils removed. Had she opted against this operation, I would not have lived through what lay before me. I still feel that God was with me.

We had to take the train from St. Hubert and travel southwest to Gross-Betschkerek for the operation.

I remember visiting Mama's two cousins Nushi and Gorgi, who were married to Hungarians. One was a waiter and served us when we stopped by his workplace. I had never seen anybody dressed this way—in black coattails, a starched, white shirt, and a black tie. All these new experiences really impressed me. After all, Betschkerek was a very large city compared to our little village.

We took public transportation to get to the hospital for the operation. Upon entering the grounds of the hospital, we saw many wounded German soldiers, either sitting in the sun or being pushed around in wheelchairs. The hospital itself was understaffed and overcrowded with recuperating soldiers. Even though there was a great big red cross painted on the roof of the hospital, which meant that the building was not to be bombed, raids occurred even during the night. When this happened, everyone who could move would head for the bomb shelters. Mama was concerned that I would be left behind. So she asked a German soldier to take me with him to the shelter in the case of an attack. Fortunately, no air raids occurred while I was there.

Medical supplies were scarce. What little they had was used on wounded soldiers and not on civilians. In this respect, I was fortunate that the surgeon managed to squeeze me into his busy schedule.

I was only six, but I distinctly recall my tonsillectomy. There was no anesthesia for me. My hands and arms were tied to my body. Then I was tied to the chair I was sitting in. A large clamp was placed in my mouth, opening it wide, while depressing my tongue. What appeared to be a hammock-like contraption, acting as a catch basin, was tied around my neck and also around the surgeon's neck, who sat across from me. I was in a state of terror. I could neither move nor make a sound. It was a very painful and horrible experience, which I will never forget. Adding to my fear were the blood and the tonsils, which fell into the catch basin. Throughout the operation I was conscious and felt all the pain. I am still surprised I did not faint from all the suffering and distress.

I asked for my mother after the nurse put me into my bed. But for some reason, she was not there. Where was Mama? Why wasn't she waiting for me? Here I was, surrounded by strangers, and there was no familiar face to comfort me. As soon as I was alone, I climbed over the bed railing. Still very much in pain and bleeding from my mouth, I was crying and running down the hallway, looking for my mama. After the failed attempt to escape, I was tied to my bed, after which I just had to take things as they came. I missed my mother's comforting nearness, and I did not understand why she was not with me. I eventually recovered completely from this frightful and terribly painful ordeal.

Years later, I asked Mama what happened the night she walked out on Tata and left me behind. She was obviously uncomfortable that I remembered anything about the incident.

Once she told me that my father hit her, nothing else. One time, when she was upset with me, she quipped, "Yes, and I had to endure all those beatings because of you." When I enquired about what happened, her answer was, "I wanted to take you to the doctor and have your tonsils removed." This made no sense to me. This incidence occurred in early spring 1942. Why did she not take me for surgery after my father left in April 1942? Instead, she waited more than two years to have my tonsils removed. Her answer: "I could not get the doctor I wanted."

In retrospect, I can only assume what happened between my parents. I never saw my father intoxicated when I was a child. I know Tata was a sensitive, gentle, and kindhearted person. He resented being married to an immature and self-centered wife, who always placed her own mama's wishes first. He actually referred to himself as "the fifth wheel in the wagon." It was only after he had too much to drink that he became angry and belligerent. I did not like it when I saw him this way. But his anger was always directed toward his wife and her dependency on her mother.

I rather doubt my father was intoxicated when this "beating" took place. I assume he slapped her in the face after she said some very unkind and unloving words about me. You see, my mother's greatest character deficiency was lack of empathy. She was unable to put herself in someone else's shoes, and that resulted in some heartless responses.

Of course it is unacceptable for a man to physically abuse a woman or intimidate her. But something my mother did or said about me upset my father very much.

I have often wondered what would have happened to my parents' marriage if World War II had not happened. The long separation and many hardships encouraged them to give their marriage a second chance.

CHAPTER 9

A Driving Snowstorm, January 1944–Summer 1944

I have tried to keep my memoirs in chronological sequence. However, the two previous chapters should not be separated. Part of this chapter actually happened six months prior to my tonsillectomy.

This is the one wartime story my father told me. He spent his entire military service during the war in Yugoslavia.

His orders were to move forward in the mountainous regions of Serbia. His unit had been on the march all day. He was carrying his heavy backpack and all other needed equipment. The steep terrain was difficult for my father, and he became very tired. Tata had spent his entire life on a level plain. Then a violent snowstorm with a driving, cold wind hit the moving troops. He started to fall behind. Totally exhausted, he stumbled along by himself. Through the blizzard, Tata saw flares shooting up in a distance, but he did not know if they belonged to his German unit or the enemy, the communist partisans. He had reached a point where he was ready to give up; he just could not go on anymore.

Then he remembered that this day was January 16, my birthday. He pictured me in his mind as I had been when he saw me last, and he began to pray. He asked God to keep him alive so he could see me again. With new determination, he kept moving.

Then he saw a light flicker in the distance, through the storm. At this point of his exhaustion, he did not care anymore who was in that little shack. He walked toward the light, ready to die if it was the enemy. But thank God it was the Germans, who took him inside to warm up. After he rested, he was able to rejoin his unit.

What touched me deeply was that in a time of great distress, he thought of me, his daughter. He did not ask to see his wife again, nor his infant son. I believe my father's desire to see me again gave him the strength and determination to keep moving. God granted his intense prayer and came to his rescue. I had the impression that Tata believed it too. Even though my father did not openly show affection, in his heart he loved me. This knowledge gave me a warm and happy feeling throughout my life.

During the summer of 1944, my father was captured by the partisans in Yugoslavia and became a prisoner of war. Tata was mistreated, receiving little food and working as a slave laborer in the coal mines. Many prisoners died.

His knowledge of music saved him. In the evenings, the partisans wanted to be entertained. My father, who was able to play music from memory, was assigned by these people. This position gave him certain privileges, such as less severe work assignments and better treatment, and most of all, more food.

For many years, my father had absolutely no idea about the fate of his family, just as we were uninformed about his survival.

CHAPTER 10

The Fate of the Danube Swabians by Late 1944

In November 1944, the National Assembly in Yugoslavia passed a law that deprived all Germans living in Yugoslavia of their citizenship and all rights attached thereto. It provided for the confiscation by the Yugoslavian state of all property portable or not of persons of German descent. It stipulated that persons of German heritage could not claim any local or state citizenship. They could not call upon the courts or state institutions for personal or legal protection. In Yugoslavia, the Germans were to be liquidated. Get rid of them; kill them. After all, the atrocities of Nazi Germany justified this. Someone had to pay for Hitler's heinous crimes.

In addition to the creation of numerous local work camps and central camps, (distribution centers), which allocated laborers to its work camps, the Tito Regime established a third category, "special camps," consisting mostly of women, elderly, and children. Molidorf, Rudolfsgnad, Gakowa, and Kruschiwl were camps where the entire village was designated as a liquidation camp. According to the book *Genocide of the Ethnic Germans in Yugoslavia,* Rudolfsgnad was the last camp to close, in 1948.

In late 1944, Stalin demanded German laborers from Romania, Hungary, and Yugoslavia for the reconstruction of Russian areas destroyed during the war. From Yugoslavia, at least twelve thousand Danube Swabian civilians were forcibly shipped to the mining and industrial areas of the Ukraine.

When the end of World War II was evident by 1944, the Russians, Poles, and Czechs had already decided upon and partially carried out the expulsion of their Germans. In Romania and Hungary, the Germans lost their property and means of production without compensation. They were also mistreated, but not to the extent of the Germans in Yugoslavia.

CHAPTER 11

Aftermath of World War II in Soltur, Fall 1944

School never started in the autumn of 1944 in our village. German troops were retreating, and the end of the war was near for us. It was an unstable and confused time.

The retreating German Army had warned us all along, "You had better flee to Germany. You do not know what the Russians will do to you."

The dilemma was to stay or flee. Winter would soon be here. Taking the train was impossible, since many central train stations had been bombed, or the rails had been dynamited by the retreating troops. That left only a horse-drawn carriage for us. But what would happen to our livestock and our property? We heard that some people were leaving, but not from our village.

My Halbherr Ota made the final decision when he said, "We have lived through one world war already. No one came into our village and harmed us. They only changed the borders." So we stayed.

Radio Belgrade still beamed out its propaganda by playing "Lili Marlen" ("The Girl under the Lantern") before sign-off in the evening. The newspaper still printed, "We will never give up the Banat." Two days later, on Friday, October 6, 1944, the Russians marched into our village.

At once, we had to turn in all radios, every weapon, all musical instruments, and all bicycles. Anyone caught keeping any of these items would be shot instantly.

Another announcement required that everyone able to work had to report to a "kolchose" an agricultural production company or collective farms to work the fields. My mother was part of those workers. Other women had to cook for the occupation forces, while some women were assigned to clean the lodgings in the village hall and other quarters.

The wine cellars in every home were still well stocked. The Russians just helped themselves and became intoxicated daily. The women and young girls lived in constant fear of being violated. A second cousin of Mama's (Tante Anusch, whose name was Anna Kuechel) spent every night in a barn loft filled with hay, with the ladder pulled away.

The Russians made house searches as they pleased. Whatever they liked, they simply took. They especially loved jewelry, including wristwatches. Other items they enriched themselves with were boots, leather jackets, suits, and fancy clothing. We lived in constant fear, never knowing what to expect of them. Any resistance would have meant immediate death.

A few weeks later, all inhabitants of our village were put into the "Wirtshaus," our community house. There we sat for two days and nights. We heard that the Serbian partisans wanted to put us on horse-drawn wagons and send us to the Soviet Union. But the Russians did not give their permission, so we were allowed to go home again, while the adults had to continue to do the fieldwork.

After the Russians pulled out and turned us over to the communist partisans, chaos began. These Serbs had a tremendous hatred for us, which they unleashed once they were in charge. One day, the Serbian communists entered every home and told the men present to step into the street. These men were mostly in their fifties and sixties, who had not been drafted and had stayed home. They marched them some six to seven miles to the dairy co-op in Kikinda. This large building had played a very important part in our daily living, but these people did not need it.

During the day, they had to repair the railroad tracks between St. Hubert and Kikinda. At night they were harassed. The guards picked them at random and killed them. But first, they had to dig a pit, then blindfold each other, and tie up their hands with shoe strings. They were chased to the pit and shot and killed. Others were beaten to the point of unconsciousness. The next day the partisans marched them, in their bloody clothes, to the work area.

From October to December 1944, at least 150 men lost their lives to brutality and torture, among them our Catholic priest. Another countryman, who was severely wounded, was able to get out of the pit later during the night. He crawled home on his knees. His mother went to get the doctor for her badly injured son. The doctor, who was a German but a partisan sympathizer, reported the young man. They came and took him away in a carriage. Later they killed him in a field.

One man was blessed to escape this nightmare. Before he was hit, he let himself drop into the pit and later went home. Disguised as an old woman, he and his family fled to Romania. From there, they made their way to Hungary, Austria, and then Germany.

These are only two examples of the horror that befell us after the war. Many books describe what happened to the population at large. Beatings, torture, rape, and killings were daily occurrences. I knew a woman who as a young girl was told to clean up a bloody room where a woman's body had been dismembered. Afterward she became a very disturbed person, ending up on disability in Germany.

On December 27, 1944, another announcement required that all men aged eighteen to sixty and all women aged eighteen to thirty had to report to the community hall. They were told to bring food supplies along for fourteen days. It was rumored that they would be heading into Serbia to finish the harvest. My mother was one of these women who had to go, as well as her brother, Jani. He had been home recuperating from war injuries. Uncle Jani was supposed to report to his unit in Werschetz in September 1944. But he could not get back, as the Russians were already there.

From our sister villages, 159 women and 14 men left in late December for destination unknown. Their major food supplies for the two weeks consisted of huge loaves of home-baked bread, smoked ham, smoked bacon, and sausage.

On December 28, 1944, I remember crying and running after my mother as she came down Main Street carrying her heavy bundles of food, clothes, and blankets. Not even a last hug was allowed between us, for the armed guards instructed them not to stop. While I was running along and crying, I kept asking my mother, "When will you come back?" She answered, "Soon." I asked again and received the same answer. But I wanted a definite date, so I asked her if she would be home for my birthday, which was only three weeks away. She promised me that she would be back for my birthday. That was a very difficult parting for me. My only comfort was that my mother would be home soon. Now both my parents were gone, and I was overwhelmed with sadness.

During many months thereafter, no communication was allowed, and neither of us had any knowledge of how the other was doing, where we were living, or whether anyone was still alive.

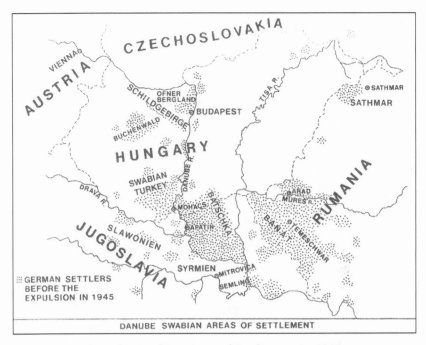

Danube Swabian Area of Settlement in 1945

CHAPTER 12

Trip to the Ukraine, December 31, 1944, to January 17, 1945

The civilian German population was sent to Russia as a workforce, compensation from Tito to Stalin for his help during World War II.

The 173 men and women carrying their heavy bundles walked the six to seven miles to Kikinda. Their destination was also the dairy co-op, where all the men had been harassed and most of them had been killed. Only a few men were left.

My mother's second cousin, Anna Kuechel, was also her close friend. They were together during their entire Russian experience. This is Tante Anusch's story (I called her aunt), as she recorded it.

Before they boarded the train in Kikinda, they were informed that their destination was Russia. Early in the morning, on December 31, 1944, the group walked to the train station and boarded cattle cars. In the afternoon, they had reached Modosch, Romania, where they were permitted to get straw from the farmers to cover the floor for their beds. Tante Anusch stated that they were nice and warm under their blankets and featherbeds. There were two sisters in the cattle car with them who did not have sufficient bed coverings and later had to get their legs amputated up to the knees due to frostbite.

During the night they reached Temeschwar, Romania, where they loaded up more food supplies for the people in charge of the transport, but nothing for the occupants in the cattle cars.

When they arrived in Transylvania, they stopped for the day. They were instructed to elect a trustworthy representative for the group of thirty women in their rail car. While they were standing there, out of nowhere appeared a train on the rails next to them. This train carried Russian replacement troops to the front line. The women peeked through the tiny windows of the cars and were seen by the soldiers. All the doors were locked from the outside, even the troops' rail cars. But as soon the men saw the young women, they went wild. They were howling and pounding on the walls. The women were terribly frightened and started to pray. The officers of the women's transport instructed them to remain as quiet as possible, wanting to protect the females. The entire group prayed their rosaries and asked God to protect them. It was a great relief for the women when the troops' train finally left.

Jaschi, Romania, was the railroad terminal where they transferred to the Russian rail cars. The tracks of the Russian railroad system were spaced farther apart than the rest of the European railroads. Supposedly, the czar had said that he did not want to be invaded by a train full of Prussian soldiers, so he had a different railroad system installed.

Now they were about eighty people in one railroad car, men and women together. The cars were double-deckers, for sleeping on the top and the bottom. No one could stand up anymore. During all this time, they never had any warm food. But they improvised. Somehow, they found some empty tin cans. When they were allowed to step out, they heated up some water for warm tea.

When the train stopped in Ploeschti, an area with large oil fields, they refilled their bottles with water, which contained some oil. Many of the women came down with a bad case of diarrhea. The train would stop during the day for the people to relieve themselves. What a misery that was, Tante Anusch said. It was so embarrassing, going to the bathroom in open country, men and women together, with no privacy. On the way, one man died. Two women in their car were very ill and died when they reached Russia.

Once they were in the Ukraine, they were permitted to leave the doors open, and they could see the countryside. It was winter and there was snow as far as the eye could see. The land was flat and sparsely populated, with only a few villages. Thus, they traveled until January 17, 1945, and almost three weeks had passed.

Early on January 18, they were told to leave the rail cars. They had to line up in rows of four and start marching. Only a few of the railroad cars were emptied of people, and the rest of the train continued on. My mother and Tante Anusch had reached Krivoj Rog, Ukraine, in the Soviet Union.

CHAPTER 13

The Expulsion, Camp Charleville, April 1945–October 1945

In the spring of 1945, a task force was needed once more to work in the fields. This time Aunt Eva (Uncle Jani's wife) was in line to go, but she was eight months pregnant. Someone in the family had to replace her. My fifty-year-old Halbherr Oma, who took care of us, had to be the substitute.

It was very common for several generations to live in the same house. However, each family had their own private entrance and apartment. We had such an arrangement in my grandparents' house. Therefore, Aunt Eva was able to look after Ota, my brother, Toni, and me, as well as her son, Nikolaus. She cooked for us, did the laundry, and took care of our needs.

A month later, in April 1945, my aunt's father, Peter Perreng, came rushing into our house and informed us about what was happening in our village. Early in the morning, the partisans started to enter each home in Soltur. They told everyone to drop what they were doing, get out of the house, lock the door, and give them the key. The people were being assembled on the street. My aunt's father told us to dress in several layers of clothes because no one was allowed to carry anything out of the house. I remember being bundled up in two sets of underwear, two pairs of stockings, two dresses, and my best coat. My aunt also put a cigarette lighter into my top dress pocket. She felt that we may need it to start a fire for cooking or to get some heat.

After the partisans demanded we leave our home, we never saw the house again.

All the inhabitants of Soltur were marched with armed guards to Charleville, a ten-minute walk, where the homes had been previously cleared out. The people of St. Hubert and Charleville joined us as well, totaling around three thousand souls. We learned that the entire contents of the homes had been removed and stored in a central area, which we were prohibited to enter.

When we arrived in Charleville, everyone was strip searched. A Serbian woman took away my indispensable cigarette lighter. All of us were terrified of these people who treated us so harshly, and if anyone dared resist, they were beaten or killed.

Our quarters were the emptied homes in Charleville. Every room was assigned between twenty to thirty people, depending on the size. The straw piles in the backyard of the farms were untouched, so we were told to get straw for our beds. The entire floor was covered with straw, leaving only the entrance and middle open. We were given some blankets, but not enough to cover the straw and ourselves. On cold nights our extra clothes were used as covers. It was difficult for me to fall asleep on the straw, which tickled and made me sneeze due to the dust and loose particles.

When my aunt went into labor, she was placed in a separate house to give birth. On May 2, 1945, with the help of a midwife, she gave birth to a little girl, who was named Anna, after her Halbherr Oma, and nicknamed "Anni." I was allowed to visit her and see the new baby.

On May 8, 1945, World War II ended with the surrender of Germany, but we had absolutely no knowledge of the outside world, since all news was kept from us.

Beginning in the summer of 1945, the partisans brought in their own people from the Balkans to occupy our homes. After the Russians had taken their share, the rest of our possessions were divided up and distributed to the new inhabitants.

Our Marx Oma was also in Charleville but not living with us. Shortly before World War II ended she worked for a retired, widowed, and fairly well-off farmer in St. Hubert. His name was Hans Schoen. She was his live-in housekeeper. This was her way of supporting herself after Tata had been drafted into the German army. Now in Charleville, she still took care of him, since he was in poor health.

For personal hygiene, we washed ourselves daily at the well in the yard, but without soap. Soap and wash powder were not available to us. Still, we were permitted to heat up water outside to get a sit bath in a tub. Once a week, my aunt washed our dirty clothes by hand in the evening, so they would dry overnight and be ready for the next day. With no indoor plumbing, all of us had to use the outhouses. The great number of people crammed together made the small structure a very busy place.

Our food was prepared in a central kitchen, to which we walked three times a day to collect our meager portions. On the menu was potato soup without salt or seasoning, just water and potatoes boiled together. As far as I can remember, this is all we received for six months. With one meal we were given a slice of cornbread, which had been prepared with some salt. However, this was impure sodium sulfate, which was used to make soap and paper pulp. Cooking salt was precious to nonexistent.

Throughout our stay in the camps, we never had any meat, fat, salt, sugar, seasonings, or dairy products, except a blue-tinted powdered milk later on. Needless to say, many older people and the very young quickly became ill and died. My great-grandmother Elisabeth Halbherr (my mother was named after her grandmother), who at ninety-one was still able to hoe the vineyards in the hot sun, soon died from this diet. She had given birth to ten children, of which only three saw adulthood. Her daughter, Theresia Adams, my grandfather's sister, soon died as well.

At least two hundred people died in those six months in Charleville. They were not buried in our cemetery. Instead, the partisans threw them in unmarked graves on the outskirts of the village. Later, the partisans leveled our cemetery to the ground, after they opened up the vaults and plundered the jewelry and gold teeth off the corpses. They used the marble and valuable stones from our cemetery and from our dynamited church to build themselves a new civic center.

Some caretakers were left behind in the villages to look after the remaining livestock. My Halbherr Ota was in charge of taking care of some hogs and chickens in Charleville. Besides feeding the animals, he also had to collect the eggs, which were picked up daily by the Serbian communists. He kept some eggs for himself and other family members. I had to sneak there to see him because we were not allowed to be in that part of the village. Ota would give me raw eggs for some additional nourishment. The eggs had to be consumed raw because no cooking was permitted. Our wood-burning stoves surely would create smoke, a dead giveaway. All of us were being watched, and we had to be very careful. If caught, Ota and I would have been beaten for breaking the rules. Most likely he would have been imprisoned as well.

I do not know for how long I was able to secretly meet my grandfather. But one day he was gone. I was devastated and full of guilt. Did I do something wrong? Just like we had no knowledge of where our Halbherr Oma was or what she was doing, so my grandfather disappeared from my life too.

Years later I learned that some distant family member had turned him in to the partisans. His crime was that he had buried our valuables and family jewelry in our vegetable garden. He also had taken some smoked meat to eat. My grandfather was severely beaten and thrown into a dark root cellar filled with ground water. There he was kept in solitary confinement for weeks.

One day my cousin Nikolaus and I decided to sneak out of Charleville to see our old home village, Soltur. We did not dare use the connecting roads. Instead we wandered through the back vineyards, which had been neglected this season. The few grapes we found we consumed. We ended up in the backyard of my Marx grandparents' house number three. The vegetable garden was overgrown with weeds, but the old apricot tree offered some ripe fruit. Nikolaus climbed the tree and tossed me the honey-sweet and great-tasting treat. We really had our fill of apricots that day. Oh, how lucky we were not to get caught. My cousin, however, does not remember this incident.

We remained in camp Charleville for six months, from April 1945 to October 1945. My three-year-old brother, Toni, and I, age seven, stayed with our Aunt Eva, her son, Nikolaus, age ten, and baby Anni.

I missed my family members who had disappeared from my life—Tata and Mama, and Halbherr Oma and Ota—but the worst part was not knowing if they were still alive and if I would ever see them again. Yes, I did miss my primary caretaker the most, my mama.

CHAPTER 14

Krivoj Rog, Ukraine, January 1945-August 1946

My mother and Tante Anusch had arrived in Krivoj Rog, a city spread out over a large area. After walking for about thirty minutes, they saw nothing but large blocks of apartment houses. Each was four stories high, with twenty huge windows in front. Each window had three sections, of which two were boarded up and the third contained a glass pane. The windows could not be opened and were covered with a heavy layer of ice.

The building they lived in only had small rooms. Each room contained six to seven iron beds. After three days, they received straw and bags. They stuffed the bags with straw and used them as mattresses. This way the beds were more comfortable. Most still had blankets from home to use as covers. Their food supplies from home were almost gone.

After two days Mama and Tante Anusch had to report for work. Wherever work needed to be done, that is where they sent the convoy.

First they had to clean streets. Then they had to dig a pit to store ice. That was nice, because soon they were below the surface and protected from the icy wind, while their supervisor was freezing on top of the pit. Next they worked as plasterers. This too was nice work in a house, which protected them from the bitterly cold Russian winters. Fortunately, the women brought warm winter clothing along from home. They had to do piecework and lived up to the Russians expectations.

When the Russians opened up a kitchen in their building for the people living nearby in the camp, ten women from Soltur applied for a position and were all accepted. It turned out to be a great blessing because the other women had to walk forty-five minutes to get to their jobs. These women worked in the nearby iron-ore mines. They returned with red hair, red skin coloring, red clothing, and red shoes. These women had a very hard time working as slave laborers.

In the building where my mother and Tante Anusch lived, there was a bath attendant, a locksmith, a tailor shop, a shoemaker shop, three hairdressers, a first-aid station (without any medical supplies), and a laundry. They also had a camp interpreter; his name was Moskaljuk and he came from Cernovcy, a city in Bukovina. In their building were people from the Banat, Transylvania, upper Silesia, and Hungary. Also, ladies and gentlemen who entertained the German soldiers during the war and were close to the front line had become captives of the Russians.

Until they had a kitchen in their building, all of them had to walk a long distance to eat. There was an inspector who made sure everything ran smoothly because of the limited space in the dining hall. He ran around shouting loudly, "Eat quickly and go quickly." He was a short man, supposedly from the southern regions, and he was Jewish.

Once the ten women from Soltur worked in the kitchen, they had a better life than the other people. In the beginning though, the crew had a very bad boss. She hated them deeply and called them "parasites." The women had to get up at two a.m. and mop the hallways. The building had two end doors and two side doors, but only the empty frames were standing, no doors. It was bitter cold outside. As soon as the women put down the wash rag, it became frozen and stiff. Their hands became raw and cracked. The next morning at inspection time, the women wept and showed their sore hands to the officer, who felt sorry for them and wept with them. Shortly thereafter, this supervisor was replaced with a new boss, Maria Petrowa. She was Jewish and was also strict, but she did not abuse the women. The women also had ten officers, one commander, and many guards (even female guards) in their building, and they were watched.

So winter passed. By the middle of March, many became ill. Tante Anusch came down with typhoid fever and had spots on her body. After spending two days at the first aid station, a truckload of sick women were transported to the hospital. They were placed into an unheated room. In the middle stood an iron stove and some iron beds. The beds were bare—no mattresses, no pillows, no covers. Finally, someone lit a fire in the stove, which threw off a little heat. The sick women were exhausted and found no rest on the hard iron beds.

The next morning, they were told to get a bath. That was a very sad experience. The room they entered did not resemble a bathroom. There was a washbowl to wash the face, hands, and feet. Next they were asked to undress since they slept fully clothed to keep warm. Afterward they received men's pajamas. Then the nurse came with a huge pair of scissors and cut off their hair, until their heads were completely bare. Tante Anusch felt that was one of the saddest things that happened to her, and she was crying. She was only twenty-four, yet she looked hideous.

Next they were placed into a room with four beds, one in each corner. This time the iron beds had a sack of straw and a blanket, but each bed had to be shared by two females, leaving one bed empty. After two days, the empty bed was occupied by a Russian male of about fifty years. He was surprised that he had to share the room with women. Tante Anusch, who spoke Serbian, was able to communicate with him and learned he had been in World War I, in Dubrovnik. Later his elegantly dressed wife came to visit him, and she asked her husband, "What young men do you have here?" She thought they were all young men, for they all surely looked that way.

By the beginning of April 1945, the recovered women returned to the camp. The ladies felt better, even though they never received any medication for their illness. They still were kept in separate quarters in the camp. This is where Tante Anusch had a bad relapse. She and other sick people from the camp were transferred to a quickly prepared house for the ill. Tante Anusch was unable to walk and had to be carried on a stretcher by four men, who themselves were sick. The house they stayed in had no bathroom, so they had to use a bucket. Tante Anusch was very weak and had to be helped by two people to get to the bucket. Since she had diarrhea, she needed a lot of help.

All her girlfriends were very worried about her. In particular, her cousin Erschi (my mother) took good care of her. My mother prepared special dishes for Tante Anusch in the kitchen. The women, who worked outside the building where my aunt stayed, would bring the food along. With the little treats and with God's help, she was nursed back to health. Once again, she received no medication for her illness.

After she was released, she returned to the kitchen. But many changes had occurred, and some women had been given new work assignments in the factories. Tante Anusch's new job was to keep the fires going under two big kettles and one little one. She had very little fuel, and what there was happened to be wet. Often she had only wet sawdust, which produced only smoke, so she came down with smoke inhalation symptoms.

Once, when she simply could not get the fires going and the food was not being cooked, Tante Anusch called her supervisor. She in turn ordered the men to take the benches from the dining hall and chop them up. While the men were doing the job, they laughed and had a lot of fun. Later, when inspection came, it was time to count the tables and the benches. Maria Petrowa placed the stools from the kitchen (they sat on them to clean the vegetables) in the place of the benches. The commissioner asked her, "Why are they so small?" She answered, "They shrank, they dried out." In all their misery, they still had something to laugh about.

The work in the kitchen was a seven-day job. After a while, they would get one day off during the week. Women who worked in the kitchen tended to get favorable treatment. So it was that during the summer of 1945, four women received special permission to go into the city after each was paid a small wage, (all total they were paid three times). They walked for about thirty minutes across meadows, fields, and small suburbs. The city itself had century-old buildings and nice streets with trees, but everything looked old. They saw very few businesses but discovered a beautiful park with benches, where they rested. At the end of the park they saw a movie theater. Sitting across from them were two women with similar hairstyles to theirs. Russian women wore their hair differently at that time. When they asked the two ladies about the movie, they encouraged them to see it. These two women were from the Ukraine, but closer to the Black Sea. They had to stay in Krivoj Rog to work, so they could not go home. They even spoke a little German, since they were part of the forced labor in Germany.

The four ladies went to see the movie and sat toward the rear of the theater. They were surrounded by young boys up to the age of about sixteen. It was an inflammatory film, portraying the Germans' terrible behavior while occupying the Ukraine. Shocked, the ladies whispered to each other.

The young boys went wild, stomping their feet and raising their voices, drowning out the sound of the movie. When they noticed that these women behaved differently, the situation became nasty. They screamed, "These are Germans too!"

Everyone took notice of them, and they began to attack them with their fists. Their heads and backs were pounded as they scurried from the theater. The women started to run as fast as they could while the howling crowd followed them. Since they had been to the city before, they knew that right around the corner was a little store owned by a Jewish man. This is where they headed. Some of the boys were right behind them and kept attacking. But the kind store owner intervened, leading them into his store and locking the doors. Thank God they escaped this great danger. After waiting for about one hour, when everything was peaceful outside, the women left. They considered the store owner their guardian angel.

There was a warehouse where the food was stored. For breakfast the women had cabbage soup or borsch, a Russian vegetable soup. The soups always tasted sour, as sauerkraut was one of the main ingredient. For breakfast they also had *rasolik*, another sour soup but prepared with pickled tomatoes and other vegetables. Very seldom were they served any potatoes during that time. At noon, they received the same soup and a tablespoon of barley with a little side dish. For supper they had the same soup, one tablespoon of barley, and a salad. There was a time when their breakfast consisted of a salad and tea. All the camp inhabitants were undernourished, with bloated bellies. All the food they received was too salted, too sour, and the servings too small.

The following year, 1946, the Russians renovated the windows. They also installed heat, put doors into the empty frames, and installed shower rooms in the basement. However, there were no toilets in their building, so they built two sheds, one for females and one for males. During the summer, they often had no water. Then water had to be fetched in pails from quite a distance away.

Tante Anusch would often talk about her children Maria and Anton (Toni). But she mainly focused on her younger son, who was about four at the time. She did not do it consciously but felt that he would have a rougher time than her daughter, who was by then already eight. Her feelings were later confirmed.

It was a great joy to get unexpected mail, which their commander passed out to them. Tante Anusch received news from her husband that he was a prisoner of war in Yugoslavia and that their children were in a state-run orphanage and had been given new identities. She was overjoyed to hear that her husband was still alive, but the news about her children brought her great sadness.

Even though she answered back, her husband never received her mail. It was not until she had written her nineteenth letter to him that he received finally news from her.

My mother also remembered the address of my uncle and aunt in Chicago, Illinois. She was able to get in touch with them by mail due to the help of the American Red Cross. Don't forget, the United States and the Soviet Union were allies during World War II and at that time were still on friendly terms.

CHAPTER 15

Starvation in Camp Molidorf, October 1945–April 1947

In October 1945, armed guards walked us from Charleville to a more central liquidation camp named Molidorf. This was a fifteen to twenty mile walk to the southwest. But before we left Charleville we were strip searched and left with only one set of clothing.

Molidorf was a much larger village than where we came from. It had been a community of Danube Swabians, with about twelve hundred inhabitants. While we were there, it was home to between five and seven thousand people, mainly women, children, and the elderly. Some late arrivals to the camp were even housed in stables due to the overcrowding.

I distinctly remember the colorful leaves on the trees as we marched, exhausted, into Molidorf. I still can picture the house we were assigned to. It was on a side street, the second house from the end of the village. We, my brother Toni and I, were with Aunt Eva, her son, Nikolaus, and baby Anni. All of us had to share the room with at least twenty other people, mostly children. I do recall the name of one of the girls in our room, Veronika Stein, because I liked her first name. She was born in St. Hubert, one of our sister villages.

Our assigned room was empty, except for the straw on the floor—our beds for the night. The built-in ovens and cooking stoves had been destroyed, and many windows were broken. No fire of any kind was permitted in any room, to avoid house fires. Even during the very cold winter of 1945-46, we had no heat. How did we survive this ordeal? I can only guess that the body heat from more than twenty people crammed into a small place allowed us to get through the winter.

Without any heated water for bathing and no soap, washing our few clothes became a challenge. Soon we became infested with body and head lice, which bit us and sucked our blood. Not only did they suck our blood, they also left us itching and scratching our skinny bodies.

Another pest was the flea, which lived in the straw. This is a small, flattened, wingless insect with large legs adapted for jumping. The adult parasite is also a blood sucker. In other words, our environment was filled with undesirable parasites plaguing our undernourished bodies.

Adding to our woes were rats and mice. They too were living with us, scurrying around, looking for food. I heard stories of hungry rats gnawing on sleeping people and infecting them with diseases. At times I was afraid to go to sleep on the floor.

Our food was prepared in a central kitchen, in many huge kettles. Long lines of people would wait patiently, three times a day, for their meager portions. We never received any meat or dairy. All the food was tasteless, since it was prepared without any fat, salt, sugar, or seasoning. But we were hungry and lived from meal to meal.

I recall receiving bluish-tinted milk, with little nourishment, for the first meal of the day. The milk was made from milk powder, donated from the American Red Cross. For lunch we always received pea soup. The peas had hard, indigestible shells and were bug infested. So floating in the hot water were a few peas, the hard shells, and the black bugs—not very inviting to be consumed. But I was hungry and always ate everything, except the bugs.

For supper, we received about 150 grams of hard cornbread and some bluish barley soup. Even though the soup had very little barley, it tasted awful. I can only compare it to the taste of wallpaper paste. Even today, I get an allergic reaction if I dare to eat barley. Many times I thought about the better tasting potato soup in Charleville and how I wished I had some to eat.

My brother, Toni, had always been a fussy eater, and he complained a lot about the food. He was so undernourished that he became just skin and bones. I think he found some comfort in my presence, his older sister, who was always there for him.

Also suffering from this diet was baby Anni. My aunt kept saying, "The child needs some meat." I do not remember whose idea it was, but my cousin, Nikolaus, who was about eleven, made himself a very primitive slingshot. Armed with this homemade contraction and some pebbles, he went out into the backyard, looking for birds.

Since no fires of any kind were allowed, my aunt, with the help of other adults, erected a very crude open pit. The fire was stoked with only dry sticks and wood so it would not create any smoke. After cleaning up the bird, my aunt boiled it in a small container. Anni was the only recipient of this special treat.

During spring time, we thought of another way to fill our stomachs. Dandelions are one of the first green plants to appear. Even at home, we would eat the leaves as a salad. In Molidorf we dug up the young plants, washed them, and consumed them. Only the young leaves taste fairly good, while the older ones get quite bitter. Of course the salad lacked any taste without salt and vinegar. But we knew dandelions are quite nutritious and high in vitamins, something our diet was greatly lacking.

We heard that some people went begging for food to neighboring villages, but this was very dangerous. Molidorf was surrounded by armed guards. If caught, you were at their mercy. They could kill you on the spot, beat you severely, or torture and imprison you.

The poor diet produced many health problems, including irritated gums and rashes, and sores developed on our bodies. Many children suffered from scurvy, a vitamin C deficiency. I developed a large, pus-filled boil on the right side of my groin, which made walking painful and difficult. There were no doctors or any medical supplies. My body had to heal itself, or I would die. The boil eventually burst open and healed. It was really a miracle that no infection set in, since the wound was never treated. To make matters worse, we had no soap or warm water to wash ourselves, no privacy, our clothes were tattered, we were surrounded by dusty straw infected by lice and fleas, and last but not least, the poor diet left everyone with a weakened immune system.

No wonder the elderly and the very young were dying faster than anyone could bury them. Each day, a horse-drawn wagon came around to pick up the dead. I remember seeing the dead bodies wrapped in blankets, on top of each other, being hauled away.

Starvation and diseases caused a lot of deaths. This left many children without adult supervision. Therefore, we were moved to a different house in the village of Molidorf. My aunt was now responsible for some fifteen children. Still more people were brought into the camp. One of them was my aunt's mother, Apollonia Perreng, who also stayed in the same room with us. My Marx Oma would be coming to Molidorf later yet.

Even these deplorable conditions in Molidorf left some people able to work. Anyone able to perform a job had to report for daily work assignments. The labor of the Danube Swabians was sold by the state to local people from surrounding areas. Field hands or house servants were available for a daily fee. This rent-a-slave system indirectly benefited the able-bodied inmates of Molidorf, as they could scrounge for food. It was a risky endeavor, but hunger was an enormous driving force. Some women were able to smuggle food into the camp for their children. Many were caught and shot outright. Aunt Eva did not qualify for this workforce. She was still nursing her baby daughter.

So what did we, the children, do during our internment? I want to emphasize that no attempt was made to educate us. Since all of us were to be liquidated, why waste money on us?

How did we spend our days? We possessed nothing and were mainly left to fend for ourselves. In Charleville, we played hopscotch, played hide and seek, and made rag balls to play soccer, since we still had some energy left. But in Molidorf we were different. We were constantly hungry and fearful for our lives. We were despondent, weak, and inactive, just waiting for the next meal.

However, there were some unexpected blessings. Olga Pavecevich, a cousin of my mother, arrived one day at our camp. She was able to get a ride on a horse-drawn wagon from Kikinda. She brought us some much-needed food, like a huge home-baked loaf of bread and an entire smoked ham. Oh, how happy we were to see Olga and receive something good to eat. Olga lived with her mother, Magdalena Riha (a sister to my Halbherr Oma) and her two children Boris and Alexandra in her home. She was married to a Serbian man, who had been imprisoned in Germany after Yugoslavia surrendered in 1941. Her husband did not want to return to a communist Yugoslavia and was still in Germany. Olga, however, did not lose her property, because her husband was a Serbian.

We were so grateful for Olga's generosity. Our digestive systems rebelled, a price we gladly paid to not be hungry for a while.

By early 1946, news of our terrible conditions in the camps had reached the outside world. Many Americans became aware of the plight of their relatives living in Yugoslavia. In Brooklyn, New York, businesspeople created United Friends of Needy and Displaced People of Yugoslavia. In Chicago, Illinois, The American Aid Society was formed. My uncle, Chris Marshall, was one of the founders. With the help of the International Red Cross, care packages were allowed to enter Yugoslavia.

Later that year, even the Vatican Radio in Rome reported in six languages the deplorable treatment and conditions of the German people in Yugoslavia. The Vatican had been made aware of the situation in Yugoslavia by Professor Hans Grieser, who had escaped his camp in Neusatz and contacted church organizations.

Of course we were totally uninformed about the outside world. Can you imagine being totally uninformed and receiving a package from the United States of America? The surprise, the joy, and the doubt were great. Who was thinking of us and sending us care parcels? It turned out that my father's older brother, Chris Marx, and his family, and also my father's sister, Caroline Marshall and her family, all living in Chicago, were able to send us some much-needed food. After all the mistreatments we had received, we needed to embrace this act of kindness, and it made us very happy. To this day, I feel that these care packages helped us survive.

Actually, the parcel was addressed to my Marx Oma, but she was not yet in Molidorf. So my brother, Toni, and I, qualified as the next of kin. I remember the first package contained a three-pound can of Crisco, a big spread of Velveeta cheese, chocolate, and some other things. We really craved the fatty food—the cheese and Crisco—and spread it on our small slice of cornbread. The long-deprived nutrients did not agree with us at first. But we were so hungry we did not mind the consequences.

All these goodies we shared with Aunt Eva, her mother, and my cousins Nikolaus and Anni. We did not know if every package they sent from Chicago was received by us, but whatever came through was a blessing and lifesaver.

Sometime later, my Marx Oma arrived in Molidorf. The man she had looked after had died. Aunt Eva mentioned many times to me, "Your grandmother does not want you and your brother. She would rather care for the rich old guy, who has promised her a big reward when they get home again." They still believed they would go back home again to their house and get their property back? Unbelievable!

In my heart, I agreed with my aunt. My Marx Oma made no effort to claim us as her grandchildren, even after the man she cared for had died.

Now that Oma was in Molidorf, she went to pick up the care packages. She lived in a different house and invited Toni and me to come visit. She also shared her food with us. Needless to say, my aunt did not like this arrangement. She told Oma, since she no longer could pick up the parcels, she did not want to look after Toni and me any longer.

Also around that time the partisans decided to remove all the children who lived in Molidorf without any adult blood relatives.

We heard that my name and my brother's were on that list. My aunt, who had married into the family, was not considered blood related. The knowledge that we were to be placed into an orphanage finally motivated our Marx Oma to claim us as her grandchildren.

This is also what happened to Tante Anusch's children Maria and Toni, and many other Danube Swabian children. They were assimilated with the communist Serbian culture.

Not only were we able to receive care packages, but mail was allowed to reach us. For the first time in almost two years, in late 1946, we had a letter from my aunt Caroline in Chicago. She informed us that my mother had been in Russia but now was living in East Germany. She also was contacted by my father, who was a prisoner of war with Tito's partisans in Semlin, Yugoslavia.

We were overjoyed to hear that my parents were still alive. We also learned where they lived, and there was new hope that in the future we may be reunited again.

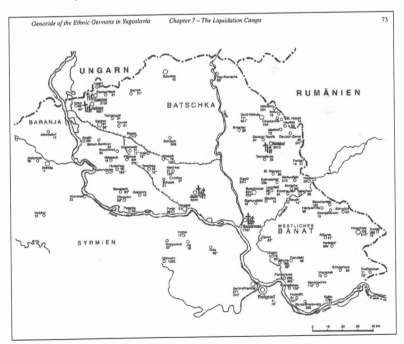

Genocide of the Ethnic Germans in Yugoslavia   Chapter 7 – The Liquidation Camps   73

Cross Symbols: The Liquidation Camps in Yugoslavia with more than two thousand casualties, recorded by names

CHAPTER 16

Internment in Rudolfsgnad, October 1945–March 1948

Originally, the town of Rudolfsgnad had 3,200 inhabitants. After it became an internment camp, it averaged 17,200 internees, with a maximum of 20,500 people. The main causes of death were starvation, typhus, and malaria.

You may recall that in March 1945, my Halbherr Oma had to take Aunt Eva's place because she was eight months' pregnant. Oma joined other Danube Swabian women and men who had to work in the fields in other parts of Yugoslavia. The state now owned all the confiscated land of the Danube Swabians, and they needed a labor force.

By autumn 1945, Oma ended up in the liquidation camp of Rudolfsgnad.

My Halbherr Ota, who had given me the raw eggs in Charleville and was imprisoned in a root cellar was also sent to Rudolfsgnad. So both my grandparents came to be together.

Rudolfsgnad had a major problem with its water supply. The water, coming from shaft wells, was inadequate for the huge number of people present, so much so that in winter, they melted the snow for cooking and washing. The rest of the year they drew water from ditches and pits.

My grandparents shared a room with twenty to thirty people. They had no blankets and were forced to lie on the floor, which was barely covered with straw.

At first nourishment consisted of ground corn soup, polenta mash, cornbread (all without salt), and tea. All total, each inmate received about two kilograms of raw ground corn per month. The small portions left everyone starving, and they gulped down edible grasses or clover to fill their empty stomachs. Some of the starving people became blind or went insane and fell into a stupor for a few days, until they fell asleep and died.

Stray cats and dogs were butchered and eaten. Many prisoners came down with diarrhea and dysentery and never recovered.

The deplorable hygienic conditions, combined with the meager food rations, contributed to the spread of the epidemic. Early in 1946, many camp occupants developed spotted fever, which quickly spread. More than six thousand people died, almost a third of the total population in the camp.

Finally, the authorities became alarmed and sent a medical team to investigate. Quarantine was declared and the camp was sprayed with DDT powder.

Afterward, the food rations somewhat improved and the inmates were given pea and barley soup, like we received in Molidorf.

Leaving the camp was strictly forbidden. If caught, the person was executed.

Ota and Oma lived completely isolated in Rudolfsgnad and had no knowledge of any of their family members, which was very difficult for them.

My Halbherr grandparents actually stayed in this death camp until it closed in spring 1948. Anyone who survived this horrible place was grateful to be alive, including my grandparents.

CHAPTER 17

Going Home—Where Is Home? 1945-51

During the summer of 1945, Marshall Tito of Yugoslavia, had visited Stalin in the Soviet Union. At that time he renounced all the Germans, who were serving as forced laborers in Russia. He simply stated that the Germans from Yugoslavia were people without a state, so Stalin could do with them as he pleased. All this was published in the Russian newspapers, which was shown to the women. Since my mother and Tante Anusch were able to read the Cyrillic alphabet, they understood everything.

But Stalin said, "What am I supposed to do with sick people?" So he released the sick laborers and sent them to East Germany.

Meanwhile, thousands of kilometers away from my grandparents, my mother was facing her second winter in Russia. Tante Anusch stated that the second winter was much better for the women who worked in the kitchen. But the people who worked outside still suffered a lot. What gave everyone strength was the hope that they would be going home one day. During September 1945, the first transport of sick people went home. But where was home? The women did not know where the train of sick people was headed.

For the second sick transport in September 1946, only two women from Soltur were on the list: their cook, Maria Kuechel, a sister-in-law to Tante Anusch, and Erschi, my mother.

Their supervisor felt that Tante Anusch was sick too, but her name was not on the list. The supervisor pleaded with the deciding commission, made up of doctors and military officials, to declare Tante Anusch sick. Even though she was not put on the list of people to go home, her boss said, "You are going home." But first she sent her to collect her wages. Tante Anusch was given two hundred rubles, a lot of money. While she was in the camp, she was paid only three times. When she came back to her room, my mother had packed up her few things too. Tante Anusch stepped into rank with the other ladies, and they marched to the railroad station. This happened on September 17, 1946, after spending twenty months in the Russian labor camp.

As soon as they arrived there, they had to line up before the last military commissioners checked them over. Those women, who looked healthy to them, were asked to step back and return to the camp. That was a trying experience that caused many women to tremble.

Fortunately, the three women from Soltur passed inspection. They were counted off into cattle boxcars. They really felt blessed because the Russians had installed a toilet in the middle of the car. After cutting a hole in the floor, they placed a primitive stand on top with a seat opening.

The next day the sick transport left. Tante Anusch and my mother had to help out in the kitchen, until they reached Brest-Litovak, the terminal between Russia and Poland. There they were transferred into European railroad cars. This was an enormously huge railroad station. For eight days they were driven back and forth at the station. During this time they were able to talk with German prisoners of war who worked there. Also, Tante Anusch was able to buy a Red Cross postcard. That was the nineteenth correspondence she mailed to her husband, Andreas, who worked in a copper mine in Bor, Yugoslavia. They traveled across Poland, passed Warsaw, and headed toward East Germany. When they arrived in Frankfurt/Oder, the Russian guards were still with them.

Once in Frankfurt, they were put into a camp again to delouse them. Fortunately, they did not have any lice. They had to remove all their clothes, which were sent to a fumigation center. Then they were allowed to take a long shower.

An elderly man who was in charge asked, "Young women, are you all pregnant?" They answered, "None of us is expecting." Their bloated bellies, which were caused by their poor diet, had misled the old man.

Then they were released from the camp with a discharge certificate. Next, all of them were sent to the state of Thuringia, East Germany, into quarantine. This precaution was done to prevent the spread of contagious diseases. They spent fourteen days in Ilenau. From there the women were sent to different towns or villages. Tante Anusch preferred to go to a farm in a village, but my mother picked a bigger town. The three women from Soltur were sent to Arnstadt, where they stayed with Frau Pressel. Poor Frau Pressel was deeply dismayed when she saw the three ragged women. They had hardly anything to wear, without even a pair of stockings or a small handkerchief. Tante Anusch found work in a cap factory, while my mother worked in a dress factory. Maria left fourteen days later for West Germany to be with her husband, who lived in Baden-Wuerttemberg.

When Tante Anusch took her Russian rubles, her wages, to a bank in Arnstadt, the bank teller was flabbergasted and wondered from where she had gotten this money. She did not know that it was illegal in 1946 to have rubles in East Germany, so she explained that this money were her wages for her forced labor, and she even produced her discharge papers. They kept her discharge papers and told her to return in two days. When she returned to the bank, the teller exchanged the money without any problem.

During the month of March 1947, Tante Anusch became very ill with pleurisy. The doctor wanted to admit her to the hospital, but my mother did not agree to it, and Tante Anusch did not want to go either. Maybe their bad experience in Russia's hospital had something to do with that decision.

My mother cared for Tante Anusch. She came home during her lunch break, changed her wet nightgown, and fed her. That was a very long and nasty illness.

When Tante Anusch started to feel better, she received a letter from her brother, Toni. He was a prisoner of war in Italy and was held by the British. He wrote that he would be discharged shortly and wanted to come to be with her, since their mother was in the annihilation camp in Rudolfsgnad, Yugoslavia. My Halbherr grandparents were also occupants of the camp.

This news prompted the two women to cross illegally into West Germany and head south to Bavaria. They did not want Toni to come to the Russian zone. The women found work in the B. M. Werke in Karlsfeld, near Munich. Toni joined them a week later. Now it was June 1947.

My mother parted ways with Tante Anusch and accepted a job in Haslach, near Traunstein, as a cook. Her cousin Anna Blassmann, sister to Olga Pavecevich, arranged the employment for my mother. This was also the news that reached us, via airmail from the United States.

I have mentioned before that Tante Anusch's children Maria and Toni Kuechel were without adult family members and therefore listed as orphans in Molidorf. They were placed in an orphanage in Debeljotsch, Banat, Yugoslavia. There they were separated, since Maria was of school age, but Toni was only attending Kindergarten. Maria was taken to an orphanage in Sopotu, Serbia, where she attended school and only spoke the Serbian language.

Both Tante Anusch in Karlsfeld, near Munich, Germany, and her husband, Andreas, in Bor, Yugoslavia, contacted the Red Cross to search for their daughter, Maria. Tante Anusch's mother, Elisabeth Kuechel, was still in Ruma, Yugoslavia, working for the state, since the liquidation camps had been dissolved in March 1948. They were in luck and quickly received Maria's address. Andreas, who was a prisoner of war, was allowed to travel to see his daughter. With his signed permission, Tante Anusch's mother was permitted to take her granddaughter out of the orphanage in November 1948. Both lived in an empty chicken coop the size of a shed. Maria was able to attend a Serbian school, and with her grandmother's help, she regained her German language.

Their son, Toni, was sent with Kindergarten children to an orphanage in Skoplje, Macedonia. With Toni were two girls from our village, Erna Renje and Erna Erndt. Both Tante Anusch and Andreas had no knowledge about their son's whereabouts. They felt powerless and were at a loss as to what to do.

Through communications with relatives, they learned that one of the girls with Toni, Erna Renje, had been picked up by her uncle. This man also saw Toni and Erna Erndt in the orphanage. Again, Andreas and Mr. Erndt had to get permission from their commander to travel to Skoplje. At the ministry, they had no record of the children, but they were told to go to the orphanage. There Toni Kuechel and Erna Erndt were listed. The children were brought in for lunch, and Andreas was told to pick out his son. Andreas really did not know his son. Toni was only three months old when Andreas was drafted into the army. What an overwhelming task—take your chance, pick out your son! Mr. Erndt pointed out Toni to his father. Thank God Andreas made the right choice in May 1949.

Andreas took Toni to be with his mother-in-law and Maria in Ruma, since he had to return to Bor. Communication was very difficult, with Oma speaking German, Maria mainly Serbian, and Toni Macedonian. In April 1950 Andreas, Maria, and Toni finally arrived at the train station in Munich, Germany. Tante Anusch was unable to describe her feelings of great joy. She had been separated from her children for five-and-a-half years and from her husband for eight long and very hard years.

Tante Anusch's mother, Elisabeth Weissmann-Kuechel, was a widow when she married Andreas's father, who was also a widower. In June 1951, six years after World War II ended, she was able to join her daughter and family in Germany. What a happy family reunion after so much suffering.

CHAPTER 18

Gakowa near the Hungarian Border, May 1947–Summer 1947

Between autumn 1946 and fall 1947, the so-called white escapes were tolerated by the Gakowa camp commanders. This also coincided with the world paying attention to the terrible conditions that existed in the liquidation camps. Therefore, escape was made easier for us, but we had no knowledge of this information.

In May 1947, we were transferred in sealed and packed train cattle cars from Molidorf to Gakowa. Originally, Gakowa had some twenty-seven hundred inhabitants, but now the camp housed close to seventeen thousand people. Between early March 1945 to January 1948, there were approximately eighty-five hundred casualties, all due to starvation, typhus, malaria, and dysentery. The camp existed for thirty-three months. Although there was no fence, armed partisans patrolled the outskirts of the village. Gakowa was close to the Hungarian border, and from the beginning, many camp occupants tried to escape into Hungary. From November 1945 to March 1946, the guards were especially cruel. During those "months of death," about half the total casualties occurred.

Even though we were late arrivals in Camp Gakowa and spent only a few months there, we quickly heard about its horrible reputation. The small and tasteless portions of food were similar to what we received in Molidorf. Any stray dog or cat had been killed and eaten. The scarcity of wood to prepare the meat forced many hungry people to consume the meat half-raw, resulting in sickness and even death. The children's hospital was so overcrowded that three to four children had to share one bed. Of course without any medical help and little food for these starving children, even their crying sounded feeble and heartbreaking. One could not help but shed tears for these helpless, suffering children.

In Gakowa, my Marx Oma; her cousin, Anna Harle; my brother, Toni; and I were together in one room with many other people. Again, our beds were the straw on the floor.

We still received the much-needed care packages from our relatives in Chicago. While Aunt Betty concentrated mainly on clothing for us and some food, Aunt Caroline's parcels focused more on food. Anything they sent was needed and greatly appreciated.

We heard that a group of men were leading Danube Swabians out of the camp at night and helped them across the nearby Hungarian border—for payment, of course. We did not have much, only one set of worn clothes on our backs, and whatever we received from the United States. We also knew of the difficulties to escape and the dangers of getting caught, even though it appeared that at the time more people were successful in crossing the border into Hungary.

My Marx Oma had frequent bouts of malaria. Her body shook with severe chills due to the high fever. This infectious disease was generally intermittent and recurrent. It was transmitted to humans by the bite of an infected mosquito. Without any medical attention, this illness left my grandmother extremely weakened, and she did not know how long she would be able to fight off this disease.

My grandmother felt that because of her age and experience with malaria, she needed to get us, her grandchildren, to our mother in Germany. She wanted us to be safe and out of this liquidation camp. I acknowledged her serious efforts to do what was best for us, her grandchildren, and I have forgiven her many years ago. Twice a year I still visit her grave in Chicago and place flowers on her headstone.

Oma met with one of the escape leaders to discuss acceptable payment. We were able to offer some of the clothing my two aunts from Chicago had sent us. Everything coming from America enjoyed high status and was greatly desired by the people living there. The payment for the three of us took most of our newly acquired possessions.

My grandmother's cousin, Anna Harle, also joined us. She had been hiding her wedding band in the hem of her only dress. The partisans were obsessed with getting gold and jewelry, so her ring was enough payment.

We had an agreement with the escape leaders: they would make three attempts to get us across the border into Hungary. If they were unsuccessful, we would no longer have any claim on them. These Serbians were our only chance to get out of the camp, so we had to trust them. The escapes were planned for the period of the new moon, or for cloudy nights, for which there would be a short notice. We were told to meet in a certain backyard, near the outskirts of the concentration camp, before midnight. They informed us that we had to stay close together, move quietly, and follow their leader—one of them would bring up the rear of the line.

A large group, perhaps eighty to one hundred people, set out on this journey. Imagine that many adults and children walking single file through rows of vineyards, into cornfields and narrow field pathways, without making any noise. The guards had disappeared when we stepped out of the camp. In our group were many young children, like my brother, who was five. These children had to walk around midnight. They were very tired, besides being weak, and they did not understand the importance of being quiet. Younger children were carried by adults and might have been asleep. Of course we knew that we were being heard, but we hoped everyone had been paid off. I was very frightened and huddled close to my grandmother in the dark while her cousin looked after Toni, who complained about being tired.

On our first attempt to escape, we did not get very far. Suddenly we were surrounded by armed border guards, who ordered us to halt. All our leaders had disappeared. We were marched to the border house and spent the night sitting in the front yard.

The fear and uncertainty of what the partisans would do to us, and the constant barrage of the mosquitoes made it a sleepless night. The millions of stars sparkled brightly on this moonless night. While I looked at the endless firmament, I asked God to help us. My mother had taught me three prayers, which I had memorized—"The Lord's Prayer," "The Apostle's Creed," and a little German prayer that went like this:

"Ich bin klein,
Mein Herz ist rein,
Darf niemand hinein,
Als Du, mein liebes Jesulein."

("I am little,
My heart is pure,
No one is allowed to enter,
But only you, my dear baby Jesus.")

The next morning, armed guards marched us back on the public road into Gakowa. The people, whom they perceived as leaders, especially men, were beaten and imprisoned. The women and us children they let go back to our common rooms. We were amazed that there was no punishment for us.

Our second attempt to escape did not fare any better. We were hardly out of the camp when the leader called, "Get back, get back." With that, the leaders disappeared. Here we were, somewhere out in a cornfield, totally confused as to where we were or what to do next. A man suggested we break up into smaller groups and separate to cut down on the noise level. He also felt that it would be wise to wait until dawn to determine our location. So we ended up with a group of twenty to thirty people, hiding in the lowest spot in a cornfield to avoid being seen. It turned out to be a very hot day, which tremendously increased our thirst. We had very little to eat and no water at all. There simply were no containers to take water along, living in a camp.

Younger children, like my brother, had no understanding of the situation, and they kept crying. In the afternoon, a severe thunderstorm with torrents of water hit us. The rain felt wonderful and cooled us off. Many of us were able to collect some water in hats or anything that could catch water for drinking. But the downpour of rain also flooded our low spot in the cornfield. The rich black soil turned into a huge mud puddle. The rest of the day and evening was most unpleasant. Wet, muddy, hungry, and shivering, we decided to sneak back into Gakowa later during the night.

Finally, the third attempt to escape was made. This was our last chance for the payment we made to the Serbian leaders. But as you may have guessed, the same problem occurred. Shortly before the border, we were told, "Get back, get back, we can't cross now." Again, we were a large group, close to one hundred people with many young children. The border patrol was heavily armed, accompanied by watchdogs, and they heard us coming. This time they didn't arrest us but let us disperse into smaller groups. In our group were mainly women, children, and a few older men.

There we sat, again in a cornfield, in the heat of the day. We had saved our small piece of cornbread for the way, but once again we had no water.

Toward noon, three Serbian men came into the cornfield pretending to hoe weeds. It would have been useless to run away. Our only cover during the day were the tall cornstalks. Not knowing what to expect, we sat there fearfully, waiting to see what was going to happen. They did not speak our Swabian dialect, but an older man who accompanied us spoke their Serbian language. These men informed us that they would help us to get across the border into Hungary. They showed us the direction we had to go and what landmarks to expect, and they told us to watch the position of the moon to determine what time to leave, since we had no watches. They also provided us with water and bread.

But for all these services, they expected payments. They spread out a sheet and asked us to donate our treasures. What an irony! Everyone expected payments from us, a people who were disowned, thrown into a camp to die, and to the end, they bled us dry. Anna Harle, my grandmother's cousin, had nothing to give anymore. All we had left were two lightweight knit tops from my cousin Carol in Chicago. They were our prize possessions. We never had anything more beautiful in our short lives. My brother, Toni, had selected a purple top with a pull string around the neck. At the ends of the string were two little bells that announced his coming when he wore it. The lemon-yellow top was given to me. Being older, I could see and understand the necessity of giving up this gorgeous top. But my brother clung to his precious possession. He cried, he fussed, he was not going to give away this piece of clothing. To this day, this incident is the only memory he has from our entire escape; it made a tremendous impression on him.

When the moon was at the designated angle in the sky, we set out on our journey across the border, which was nothing but a ditch. Finally, these three men arranged for us to safely get across the border into Hungary.

Our joy to get into Hungary was short-lived because of the constant fear of being captured and forced to return to the camp. So we had to be very cautious.

CHAPTER 19

Night Border Crossings, Summer 1947-October 1947

While the average Hungarian was not likely to bother us, we continued to move only at night because of the danger of state officials or the Red Army (the Russians occupied Hungary) detaining us. We were not safe until we could make our way, as refugees, into Austria. Our apparel gave us away as escapees, so caution was in order.

Once we were in Hungary, our group of thirty people broke up again. We still were not safe. If caught, especially in the border villages, we would be returned to Gakowa. Walking in a smaller group also drew less attention to us. The four of us—Oma, her cousin Anna Harle, my brother, Toni, and I—skirted around the nearest Hungarian village, always afraid and on guard. Some dogs picked up our nearness and kept barking, which in turn made us move even more quickly.

Once we were past the border villages, the Hungarian population was generally kind to us. Thousands of smaller groups, like ours, made their way north, toward Austria. We rested during the day, always undercover. Walking at night actually made it possible for us to use the public roads. There was not much traffic, since few people owned a car, while the horse-drawn wagons mainly traveled during the day. If we heard or saw someone coming, we still had time to hide in a ditch or a field. But we never dared venture into a town or a village, only skirted around them.

Once we caught a ride on a northbound freight train. The train was just sitting there with open doors, inviting us. I do not recall how long our ride was, but it gave us some much-needed rest, because the daily walking left us all exhausted, especially my brother, who cried a lot out of tiredness, and he needed to be encouraged to move on. I felt sorry for him, because he looked undernourished, skinny, and very weak.

Another daily concern was looking for food, water, and shelter. At times we begged for food, and if necessary we even stole fruit or vegetables from farmers' fields. We were exposed to the elements and had no change of clothes when it rained. Many times we did not have a chance to wash up in the morning, and our appearance became shabby. The stress and fear of being apprehended was always present in our minds. Thus, this journey took its toll on our overtired bodies. I have no idea how long it took us to reach the Austrian border, which we crossed illegally at night, without any problem.

In 1947, Austria was divided into four zones, just like Germany. The zones were controlled by the Americans, the Russians, the British, and the French. The Allied Forces pulled out of Austria in 1955 under the condition that Austria remain neutral.

In the summer of 1947, Austria was overflowing with refugees and displaced German people. The detention camps and all available living spaces were overcrowded. The bombed-out cities left many Austrians homeless themselves. Understandably, we were not really welcome, but we were not turned away. To our big surprise, we had entered Austria in the Russian zone. We still had not escaped the Communists' control.

The Austrian authorities found shelter for us. Anna Harle was placed with a baker in town who needed help in his shop. I remember entering the bakery and being greeted with a delicious aroma of freshly baked bread. I had not seen, smelled, or eaten fresh bread in years. But without any money, I had to postpone my desire for the bread. Yes, the Austrians did not have much to eat after the war, but they still had much more food than what we had seen in many years.

It was much more difficult to find someone willing to take in an old woman, my grandmother, with two young children. Toni was five, and I was nine. A farmer, far removed from town, gave us a room. The farmhouse was surrounded by high wooded hills, which looked to me like tall mountains. Since I grew up on flat land, these hills looked very impressive. Oma's job was to mend and sew all the clothes for the family and help in the kitchen in exchange for room and board for the three of us. I performed little chores too, like collecting the eggs from the chicken coop and setting the table.

We were so happy and grateful for the good food, the shelter, and to be safe. But what I enjoyed most was to be able to get a sit bath and get cleaned up again. We did not plan to stay there for long. Our goal was to reach Haslach, Germany, where my mother was living.

In the meantime, Oma wrote to her daughter and son in Chicago, informing them of our temporary home. They in turn always enclosed money in their letters. I do not know what the exchange rate was, but an American dollar was worth many Austrian Schillings. My mother in Germany was also informed about our coming.

We stayed with the farmer for about two or three months. It was essential to get to Germany before the winter set in. Before we left, my grandmother exchanged some dollars for Schillings to buy train tickets for the four of us. Frau Harle had a son in Germany whom she wanted to join. At that time it was still possible in Austria to cross from the Russian zone to the American zone without difficulties. Still, before the train left the Russian zone, Russian soldiers boarded the train and conducted "inspection." Anytime we saw a Communist, we were terribly afraid. How relieved we were when we finally reached the American-controlled zone in Austria. The train took us all the way to Salzburg, a beautiful city and the birthplace of Mozart. At that time our main concern was our survival; the sightseeing came many years later.

In Salzburg, we were able to stay at a transient detention camp for several days and nights. My grandmother still had some American dollars that needed to be exchanged into German Marks. But she was afraid to enter a bank. She felt that the combination of looking like a refugee and having the most sought-after money in the world in her hand might create suspicion and the authorities would apprehend her.

We met a nice lady who was very sweet and helpful to us. She informed Oma that she had been helping out many people who were in a similar situation. She convinced us that she could get more money on the black market for our dollars. Ever trusting, my grandmother gave her the money. But before she left, she treated all of us to an ice cream cone. This was the first time in our lives that Toni and I ate ice cream. What a heavenly treat! Needless to say, Toni and I loved this lady.

The next day, we waited at our designated spot to pick up our German Marks. We waited . . . and waited. We never saw this woman again. What a frustrating and disappointing experience! We were such trusting and naïve people. This left us penniless.

I need to mention that Salzburg, Austria, was very close to the German border. Refugees like us could not openly enter into West Germany. My grandmother and Frau Harle gathered information about the best way to enter Germany. By now it was October 1947. While the sun was still warm during the day, the nights had become very chilly. As you know by now, nights were the only time we could travel, except for the train ride in Austria.

This was not an easy undertaking, since we had to walk around the Untersberg, a high wooded mountain with steep slopes. We walked for hours, never seeing anyone. This kind of climbing was most difficult for the two old ladies, each one hanging on to one of us. Toni was with Frau Harle, while my grandmother tightly held my hand.

Sometime during the night we saw lights below and assumed we were in West Germany. We camped for the rest of the night on this very steep slope. I remember that Frau Harle was with Toni, perched against a tree some twenty feet above us. My grandmother and I tried to get some rest leaning against another tree below. It was a very chilly night, and all of us were freezing.

A heavy frost covered the ground when we descended the hill the next morning. The soles of my shoes were worn out and had large holes. Walking over the frost-covered meadow soaked my socks and made my feet ice cold.

We knocked on the first door in our path. Fortunately, we had arrived in Germany. The family who opened the door to us was a blessing from God. Their actions showed true compassion and Christian love. First they let us wash up and bathe our ice-cold feet. Then we received hot tea and buttered bread for breakfast. Did that ever taste delicious. They also provided us with dry socks before we left. Last but not least, when they heard of our plight of losing our money, for which we had planned to buy train tickets to get to Traunstein, they insisted that we accept the money to purchase the train fare. I will never forget these kind people, who took us in and shared with us whatever little they had themselves. I don't remember their name, nor would I ever find the house again, but every time I get to this part of my story, my eyes tear up and I get very emotional. Their kindness touches my heart, even today. What a fitting reward for all the hardships, separations, pain, and suffering we all had endured so far in our lives.

CHAPTER 20

Reunited with Mama, October 1947–Summer 1948

Germany was still recuperating from World War II. The stores did not offer much, and even if they had the merchandise, not many people had the funds to buy things. American cigarettes, coffee, and chocolates were items that dominated the black market. My teacher, Fraeulein Gall, loved coffee, but it was not available, so we sold her our American coffee for twenty Marks a can, a lot of money at the time. For us, coffee was a luxury that we could do without, since we needed the money more.

After a relatively short train ride from Freilassing, about fifteen miles, we arrived in Traunstein, a city of twenty to twenty-five thousand inhabitants, in the state of Bavaria, Germany. It was a cool October day in 1947; the trees had shed most of their colorful leaves and were almost bare. From this area, we had a view of the beautiful Alps to the south.

Once again, we had to walk to Haslach, a village about one mile from the train station where my mother worked. It was a joyous reunion with Mama, whom I had not seen for close to three years. However, my brother, who had been two years old when she was taken away, had no memory of her at all. Naturally my grandmother was relieved to turn us over to our mother. Frau Harle borrowed money from my mother for the train ticket to her son.

Mama was employed by the Gfaller family. She worked as a cook for the large household. The family was well off, for they owned a large dairy farm, as well as a grain mill and sawmill. Many of the employees received room and board as part of their payment. In 1947, Germany had an acute housing shortage, and food supplies at times were low, but at Gfallers, no one went hungry. The cows provided milk and cheese, the chickens laid eggs, and there was always flour from the mill for baking bread. Once or twice a week, they even served meat. I really appreciated all the delicious food and never had to go hungry again.

My mother prepared three meals daily for twenty to thirty people. She had only Sunday afternoons off. She certainly needed help peeling mountains of potatoes, cleaning the many vegetables, and washing big loads of dishes. The family gladly hired my grandmother to do the job—for room and board only.

As I mentioned, housing was in short supply. My mother shared a narrow room with one of the house maids. Each one slept in a twin bed. After we arrived, five people had to share this tiny room. Another twin bed for Oma and Toni was added, while I had to sleep with Mama. It was a very crowded room indeed, leaving only a narrow path to walk in the middle. But the arrangement was to be temporary, since Oma planned to join her children in the United States. We did not complain. This was heaven compared to what we had before. But most important was that we had been reunited with our mother.

The owners, however, did not like having us children around. They actually made some decisions for my mother. They wanted us to start school after the Christmas vacation, Toni in kindergarten and me in first grade. They also convinced my mother that she should place us into a Catholic orphanage in Traunstein. When it came to making important decisions, Mama was always at a loss. She tended to take the easy way out. However, Mama enquired about housing, but nothing was available.

During that time, government officials were in charge of housing. Everyone's name was placed on a waiting list. Most of the German cities had been bombed and houses were still in ruins, and the influx of millions of displaced people and refugees contributed to the existing housing shortage. My mother felt that she had no other choice and agreed with her employers. I disliked the idea very much and told her so.

After Christmas in 1947, we were placed in a Catholic children's home in Traunstein. Toni was in the boys' section, while I was in a different building with the girls. I never saw Toni during the week. We had no contact at all. Only on Sunday afternoons, when my mother came to visit or took us out for a walk or a treat, did we get together. It was a very regimented existence, with strict discipline and control. About twenty girls slept in a large dorm-like room with a nun who had her own compartment.

Everyone had to wear a uniform, which clearly identified us as belonging to the Catholic orphanage. I did not like wearing the uniform because some people looked at us with pity, while others showed contempt. I had a mother and felt I did not belong in that place.

All of us attended public schools. We had to walk through the town of Traunstein to get there. In Germany, church and state were united; religion was taught in public schools. A Catholic priest came once a week and gave us religious instructions. In Bavaria, the majority of people were Catholic. Only a small number belonged to the Lutheran faith. They were called *Protestanten*. The Lutheran children received separate instructions. It was considered a mortal sin for us Catholics to enter a Lutheran church at that time.

In January 1948, a few weeks before my tenth birthday, a nun from the orphanage walked with me to an all girls' school and registered me in first grade. Boys attended school in a separate building. I will never forget the great embarrassment I felt as I, a much older and taller girl, sat with the little first graders. The implication at that time was that I was not very bright and had failed three years of schooling. There was a stigma attached to failure in school.

It had been four years since I attended kindergarten, and of course I did not remember a thing. Complicating matters further, I entered first grade in the middle of the school year and had missed one-half year of learning the basics. But being older and more mature was in my favor. I caught on quickly in my school assignments.

But I was not very happy. Every time I saw my mother, I would beg her to take us out of the home. I wanted to be with her. After all we had gone through just to get to her, and now we were separated again.

Early in 1948, my grandmother had applied for immigration to the United States to be with her daughter and son and their families. It was only a matter of time for the approval to come through, since her children were her sponsors.

I believe my constant pressure on my mother helped her to make this decision. She finally told the Gfallers that she was taking her children out of the orphanage after the school year ended in July 1948, and that we were moving in with her. Reluctantly, the family agreed. I need to add that we were not mistreated and the food was very good. The place was very neat, clean, and well managed.

My aunts still kept sending us packages, especially clothing. I had received two very nice dresses from my cousin Carol, which were only worn on Sundays to church. During the week, the less attractive or older dresses had their turn, but for Sunday only the best wardrobe would do. The dresses were not new, but they were in excellent condition compared to my worn-out clothes. I was very proud to wear my American outfits and grateful for any gift I received.

CHAPTER 21

Closing the Liquidation Camps, March 1948

In March 1948, the communists closed the liquidation and work camps in Yugoslavia. The surviving ethnic Germans were forced to enter a three-year work contract. They still were property of the state. They had to stay with their assigned jobs and could not move about freely. All borders were strictly watched.

After three years of obligation to the state, the people were allowed to buy their freedom. First they charged three thousand dinar per person, which later went up to twelve thousand dinar per person, according to the three-sister-village book. Since none of these people had the funds to buy their freedom, it was up to the family, or relatives in Germany and Austria, to send the money for their release. First the communist Serbians confiscated all the property of the Danube Swabians. Then, while some were sent to slave labor camps in Russia, the elderly and very young ended up in liquidation camps. Those who survived still owed the state three more years of work. Afterward, when the people wanted to get out of Yugoslavia to join their families, they had to buy their freedom with huge sums of money they never earned. But the state of Yugoslavia made out just fine, getting the sought-after German Marks and Austrian Schillings.

My Halbherr grandparents were allowed to stay with Olga Pavicevich in Kikinda, while they were serving the years of their work obligation. Olga was the lady who visited us in Molidorf and brought us some food. Oma's sister, Magdalena Riha, also lived with her daughter. It was some comfort to my grandparents that they were allowed to share the house with Olga while they completed their work requirements to the state.

It was also during this time that the prisoners of war received more freedom. My father was allowed to write to us in Germany. We were very happy to hear from him and that he was well. But as a prisoner of war in Yugoslavia, his mail was still being censored.

We became very excited when Tata wrote that he had filled out papers requesting to be reunited with his family in Germany. I was hoping it would be soon. Still, I wondered if I would even recognize him. Did he change a lot? I had not seen him since he left in 1942, six years earlier. Nor did we receive any pictures of him throughout all the years. But at least there was hope that I would see him soon. That was very comforting.

CHAPTER 22

Responsibilities at a Young Age, Summer 1948–December 1949

While we were still at Gfallers in the summer of 1948, my two best dresses, my Sunday outfits, were stolen. Other items disappeared also. We did not suspect the housemaid in our room but rather the lady of the house. It was known that she had a mental breakdown. Of course we had no proof.

Only Sunday afternoons and evenings were free for my mother and grandmother, since cooking daily for a large crowd was time consuming. Circumstances elected me to do the weekly laundry for all four of us, at age ten. I did all the work, which I knew needed to be done. Without a washing machine and dryer, I washed all the soiled clothes by hand several times and rinsed them. The most difficult items to wring out were the large sheets and blankets. It took me at least four to five hours each week to finish the job. On sunny days, I was able to hang the laundry outside. On rainy days, the high attic came in handy to dry the wet clothes. Afterward came the ironing with a stove-heated iron. I never had much free time to play.

The Gfallers did let us children move back into their house, but so many things happened in our room that indicated to us we were not welcome back. My dresses were stolen, and other things disappeared.

But when my grandmother's immigration papers and other documents vanished, we had to call the police. My grandmother had to reapply for her immigration. Mama and Oma felt that someone was out to harm us in the house. The crime was serious enough not to take a chance by waiting there for anything else to happen. This incident was the last straw for my mother and grandmother, and they decided to leave.

My mother's brother, Johann Halbherr, had been reunited with his family after returning from a Russian slave labor camp. They lived in Traunsdorf, about two miles from Haslach, in temporary barracks. Their living quarters were two rooms, which housed Uncle Jani, Aunt Eva, their two children Nikolaus and Anni, and my aunt's parents. We had nowhere else to go, so they took us in. The two medium-sized rooms now had ten occupants. Obviously, this had to be temporary. My mother talked to the mayor in Traunsdorf and presented our situation. She asked for an exception to the rules, since she felt that we had a serious situation and could not remain at Gfallers.

The mayor actually pleaded with a farmer in Wolkersdorf to give up a twelve by twelve foot storage room, which was not even listed as available.

In autumn 1948 we moved to Wolkersdorf, just one mile from my uncle's barracks. Squeezed into this small room were two double beds with a table in the middle. Oma and Toni slept in one bed, while Mama and I occupied the other bed. The beds served also as the only seating arrangements while eating at the table. The used furniture was bought using my mother's saved wages.

There was a wood-burning stove that served two purposes: it cooked our meals and heated the room. The rest of our meager belongings were packed away in cardboard boxes, stacked in one corner of the room. A neater appearance was accomplished by covering the boxes with a blanket. An old chair held our portable wash basin, our only means of washing and sponging down our bodies.

The room had no plumbing. Water had to be carried in from the well. Dirty water needed to be carried outside to the backyard, where the outhouse was located.

In September 1948 I entered second grade in Traunstein, taught by Fraeulein Gall. She felt I needed the entire year to catch up on all the missed basics. Each day, rain or shine, I walked to school from Wolkersdorf to Traunstein, a one-hour walk each way.

When I look at my second-grade class picture, I see a smiling girl with braids, in the back row, my face half-hidden because I did not want to be recognized. My low self-esteem prompted me to conceal my identity.

Toni, in the meantime, went to a local grammar school in Erlstaett, only one mile away. There, Kindergarten through second grade occupied one room. Toni never liked school. This may have contributed to his just-average grades throughout the years.

My mother worked as a seamstress in a factory in Traunstein. Daily, she too walked both ways to and from work while Oma stayed home and cooked the evening meal for us. We ate a lot of noodles, dumplings, bread, and potatoes, especially potato soup, which was much tastier than what we had in Charleville. Meat was too expensive, so we could not afford it very often. Occasionally, on Sundays, we would splurge and have small portions of meat for dinner with potatoes and bread as fillers.

But soon my grandmother's immigration approval came through. In February 1949 she left for Chicago. We went with her to the train station in Traunstein. After all we had been through together, it was hard to say good-bye to her. But there was always the hope that we may join her later on in the United States. She flew from Frankfurt/ Main to Chicago.

With my grandmother gone, once again I was left to do many household chores. Mama never liked doing housework, like cooking for her family and cleaning. But she enjoyed cooking for big crowds, because of the recognition and praise she earned. Most of her life she found a willing person to take over the work she did not want to do. Now it was my turn to take over. For example, I would have dinner ready when she came home from work. Actually, she expected it from me, as she worked all day and needed to relax in the evening. But first

I had to carry the wood and the needed water inside. It was often a challenge to get the fire going in a wood-burning stove to prepare our meal. I still helped out with the weekly laundry, doing it by hand. I had to do my daily school homework, and my mother also asked me to make sure Toni got his homework done before she came home.

I was given all these responsibilities by my mother at age eleven. My entire life I tried to please her, to find acceptance and love from her. Obeying her wishes by doing her work was one way to earn her approval. So I tackled the assignments, never complaining or rebelling. I just knew my help was needed.

Over all these years, I was a comforting presence for Toni. I was his constant companion and pillar of stability. At age two, he lost his mother; four months later, his Halbherr Oma was gone. For two years there was Aunt Eva, and then his Marx Oma took us in. Finally, at age five, when he saw his mother, he did not know her. But I, his big sister, was always there and a steady support to him, throughout his tumultuous young life.

Toni did not always cooperate, and I did the only thing I knew at my tender age. I hit him on the head. He complained to our mother, but she never corrected me, never told me to stop. She did not want to be bothered, since she always had a problem with making a decision. I carried out her wishes, so she did not want to displease me and remained neutral. Toni, to this day, does not understand that our mother abdicated her role as a mother and an adult and let me, an eleven-year-old, do her job. Of course I am sorry I hit Toni, but without any understanding of the situation, there is no forgiveness from my brother.

Throughout the years, Toni and I got along well because there was always an adult present who told him what to do. When my mother put me in charge, Toni rebelled. He resented the fact that I "ordered" him around. It was painful to me when he told his side of the story to his children, who were thereafter hostile to my family and me. He claimed that I bossed him around and hit him until he fought back and pulled my long braided hair. Then I left him alone—ha, ha.

So another school year passed. My second-grade teacher felt I was ready to advance to third grade. She said to my mother, "There is nothing I can teach her anymore." At the same time, we were still waiting patiently to hear that Tata's request to join us had been approved.

In fall of 1949, I entered the grammar school in Erlstaett, where third, fourth, and fifth grades were combined in one room, with Fraulein Rainer as my teacher. The entire situation was beneficial. I heard what each grade learned and was old enough to comprehend all the lessons. I spent half a year in third grade and finished fourth grade in spring of 1950. I was eventually able to catch up with my peers in school and graduate at age fourteen from upper grade school.

But something joyous and wonderful happened in late December 1949. My father was released as a prisoner of war from Semlin, Yugoslavia. I had not seen him for seven years and eight months, close to eight years. Toni was only a two-month-old baby when my father last saw him on a short furlough. Of course Toni had no memory of his father.

My parents had been exchanging letters now for more than one year. We knew that my father requested to be able to join his family in Germany, after he was released as a prisoner of war. But no one knew when the Yugoslavian government would let him go.

I was coming home from school late in the afternoon, walking with two other friends. As we entered Wolkersdorf, I saw a man coming toward me. He looked at me and said, "Are you Lisl Marx?" Of course I was startled, but I recognized him right away. Oh, what a happy reunion that was. Such joy, expressed with many tears and lots of hugging. My father tested me by meeting me on the road first. It made him very happy that I still remembered him after all these years.

Here we were, in this tiny room in Germany, all four of us sleeping in only two beds, but we were reunited, and we thanked God for being at our side during all the separations, struggles, and hardships, sparing our lives and reuniting us as a family in late December 1949.

My father and mother, Nikolaus and Elisabeth
Marx, and me, about 1 year old

The backyard of my Halbherr grandparents in Soltur. My cousin,
Nikolaus Halbherr, 5 years old, and me, about 2 years old

My Christmas tree and wooden doll carriage at age 4

In Soltur, my brother, Toni, 1 year old, and me, 5 years old

1940 in Soltur. My Marx grandparents Anton and
Magdalena, and their youngest son, Franz, 19

Saint Hubert Church, built in 1791, destroyed
in March 1948 by Tito's Communists

1953 Schmidham, Germany. Standing L to R: Elisabeth and Nikolaus Marx; me; my brother Toni; Nikolaus, Eva, and Johann Halbherr. Sitting L to R: Lorenz and Anna Halbherr; Apollonia and Peter Perreng, Eva's parents. Center front: Maria and Anni Halbherr

Our wedding day September 20, 1958. Taken in front of 2838 N. Rockwell St. Chicago. Behind us L to R: Apollonia Perreng; Anna Halbherr; Alexandra Pavecevich; Magdalena Riha; Friedrich Wilms; and Lorenz Halbherr

Our sons Friedrich (Fred) 3½ years old, holding
Michael (Mike), 4 months old

Lindenhurst, 1967, in front of our new home
at Easter time, Fred, me, and Mike

Christmas in Lindenhurst, IL, standing L to R: Me and my
father, Nikolaus Marx; sitting L to R: Grandmother Anna
Halbherr; Mike; my mother, Elisabeth Marx; and Fred

1973 Christmas in Lindenhurst, IL, L to R: our son
Fred; my husband, Fritz; and our son Mike

1981, Fiftieth wedding anniversary of Chris and Caroline Marshall,
seated L to R: Nikolaus Marx; Caroline and Chris Marshall; Elizabeth
Marx (Aunt Betty); standing L to R: Friedrich Wilms; Carol Madden;
Elizabeth Wilms; Elisabeth Marx (mother); Elisabeth Marschall; Anna
Halbherr; Chris and Grace Marx; Judie and Anton (Toni) Marx

1982 Fritz and me at a wedding

1982, our son Fred at age 23

1982, our son Mike at age 19

Norwalk, CT, in 2000; our son Fred; grandchildren
Mina, 6 years old, and Peter, 3 years old

Fred, Mina, and Peter at the Museum of
Science and Industry in Chicago

Darmstadt, Germany 2010. Seated: Anna Kuechel (Tante
Anusch); standing L to R: her son and wife, Toni and
Rena Kuechel; daughter and her husband, Maria and
Achim Vollmeyer; granddaughter Gabi Vollmeyer

Mina, 16

Peter, 12

Epilogue

After our joyous reunion with my father, I had to sleep in the same bed with my younger brother. My parents felt that, as a twelve-year-old girl, I should sleep in my own bed, and they requested larger living quarters.

In 1950 we were assigned a three-room apartment in Schmidham, a little village, only two miles from Wolkersdorf.

In 1951 my Halbherr grandparents were permitted to leave Yugoslavia after they had completed their three-year work requirement and bought their freedom. They joined us in our apartment in Schmidham.

At the same time, my parents applied for immigration to the United States.

I was very happy to catch up with my peers in 1952 and graduate with them from grammar school. I also was accepted at a Catholic business school for girls in Traunstein, where I studied three years of English and fifteen other subjects.

By 1955 I had finished business school, and I was offered a secretarial position. At the same time, our immigration request had been approved, with my father's siblings as sponsors. On June 20, 1955, my family flew from Munich, Germany, to New York City.

We reached Chicago by train and were very happy to meet our American relatives. My first job, at age seventeen, was at a girdle factory. My wage was one dollar per hour. My father also requested that I help with paying off our immigration debt to our relatives. At the same time, I attended Schurz High School in Chicago at night to improve my English skills. I graduated three years later with a high school diploma.

I applied for a position at Prudential Insurance Company, downtown Chicago, in 1956, and was hired in their field accounting division.

Also, my Halbherr grandparents were able to join us in 1956, here in Chicago, after my parents sponsored them.

My uncle, Johann Halbherr and family, also immigrated to the United States in 1956 and lived in Chicago.

Early in 1957, my Marx Oma died. She had remarried a man she knew from at home, William Sigmund.

During the summer in 1957, my girlfriend Wilma Stafflinger and I spent a week vacation in Wisconsin Dells, Wisconsin. There I met my future husband, Friedrich Wilms, called "Fritz." He was born in Duisburg, Germany, and came to this country as a baby with his parents in 1930. He was in the US Air Force, stationed at O'Hare Field near Chicago. At that time it was a military base only.

We fell in love and were married on September 20, 1958, in Chicago. At that time, my husband was stationed at a radar station in Sault Ste. Marie, Michigan. Our first son, Friedrich Nikolaus, named after both his grandfathers, was born there on October 23, 1959.

I need to mention that my in-laws were not pleased with their son's selection for a wife. Fritz was supposed to go to Germany and let their relatives pick out a nice German girl for him. There were other incidents that clearly conveyed their message of displeasure.

In 1960, Fritz was sent to an isolated location in Labrador, Canada, for one year. Fred and I remained in Sault Ste. Marie. During that time, I was in a major accident, which totaled our car. Only I was injured with a fractured jaw.

When Fritz returned in 1961, his new assignment was at Chanute Air Force Base, Rantoul, Illinois. In 1962, I became a proud US citizen.

Our second son, Michael Anthony, was born in Rantoul, Illinois, on January 20, 1963. My brother, Toni, was Michael's godfather, so he received part of his name.

In August 1963, my Halbherr Ota was hit by a car and killed while crossing a street in Chicago. At age seventy-nine, he was on his way to work as a janitor.

A month later, my brother, Toni, married Judie Rice in Chicago. They eventually had four children.

Due to medical problems, Fritz was discharged from the US Air Force in the summer of 1965. My parents offered to help us until our new house was built. We moved into our new home in spring 1966, in Lindenhurst, Illinois.

In 1969, my father had a brain tumor removed, followed by him having a stroke, which left him disabled. My Halbherr Oma was the "real caretaker" of my father.

Also during that year, my mother-in-law was involved in a car accident and was hospitalized with a broken hip. I was accused of destroying my in-laws' mail, which never arrived. My father-in-law only wanted to see Fritz but not the rest of his family. Fritz refused to go alone to his parents, which ended their relationship.

In 1970, with Fritz's encouragement, I attended part-time evening classes at the College of Lake County, Illinois, and applied for teaching credential. I transferred my credit hours to Barat College, Lake Forest, Illinois, and finished my schooling in late 1978, at age forty, graduating in 1979 with a degree in education/psychology. My brother did not attend my graduation party. I worked at the Lake Villa School district for nineteen years as a substitute teacher.

In 1973, my uncle Chris Marx Sr. died in Florida. Also, Fritz's father died. We learned of his death from the newspaper. His sister, Marianne, also never notified us of Fritz's mother's death in 1977.

At the same time, in 1977, our son Fred graduated from high school with honors.

In 1981, Fred graduated from Northwestern and attended the University of Michigan for a master's degree in business.

In 1983, Michael graduated from high school and attended two years at the College of Lake County, Illinois, earning an associate degree in business.

My mother needed surgery in June 1985, followed by a second one in September, and the last surgery in January 1986. Each time I moved in with them to care for my father, who had developed Alzheimer's.

In April 1986, my beloved Tata died. I was heartbroken. My mother's behavior toward me changed after my father's death. She became a different person, someone I did not know—angry, short-tempered, and heartless. After my father's death and after my mother had been involved in several minor car accidents, my grandmother wanted security for the money she had given my mother. Oma picked me to carry out her wishes. In case my mother died before Oma, I was to make sure she got her money back. This was set up by a lawyer.

In 1987, Fred married Nancy Follis in New York City. Toni did not attend.

For my surgery in January 1988, my mother's behavior was so hurtful and full of retaliation that, at the age of fifty, I acknowledged to myself that my mother did not love me. I also realized that it was not in my power to put love into her heart for me. The same year my mother gave me a needlepoint picture to replace the picture my husband had given me, which I refused to do. A big conflict erupted.

My Halbherr Oma died in 1992. By then, my mother and brother were a team, working against me. My brother actually told me, "For fifty years you ran the family. Now I am taking over." I thought he was out of his mind. I need to add that my brother viewed me as the favorite of my father and my grandmother, which he resented. It is true, I was their favorite. Why? I had adopted the same philosophy, values, and outlook in life as they did. We had a lot in common, while my brother led a different and foreign lifestyle to them. As a woman I was considered the caretaker, and I helped them out much more than my brother ever did. My husband did more for my parents than my brother did at that time. But "running the family for fifty years" as an inexperienced young person was not in my power. Oma was a very strong-willed person.

I have always been interested in handwriting analysis. During 1993, I took an evening course in that subject. I found it so fascinating that I signed up with The Institute of Graphological Science in Dallas, Texas. In March 1994, I received my certificate as a certified graphologist.

June 29, 1994, was a joyous day, as our granddaughter, Mina, was born.

Three deaths in the family occurred in 1995. Uncle Chris Marshall died on January 31, Aunt Betty (Elizabeth Marx) passed away March 25, and Aunt Caroline (Marshall) followed on April 11.

Fritz and I decided to buy a bigger house. Michael was still living with us, and when Fred and family came to visit, our house became very crowded.

We built a new house in Trevor, Wisconsin, just across from the Illinois state line and moved in April 1996. During 1995 and '96, my thoughts were mainly focused on designing the house with its various activities. It actually was a great diversion from my problems with my mother.

Early in 1997, my cousin Joe Marshall passed away.

Another happy day was December 29, 1997, with the birth of our grandson, Peter.

My uncle, Johann Halbherr, died in May 1998, and his wife, Aunt Eva, passed away in December 2003.

The same year, our son Michael met Mary Peterson at work. Two years later, they became engaged.

In January 2002, my cousin Carol Madden passed away in Florida.

It also saddened me a lot to learn of the death of Tante Anusch, on December 5, 2012. I know she would have loved to see part of her story in print. This way, she will not be forgotten.

After having survived a devastating world war, I found myself in the middle of an inner "war," as I struggled for love and acceptance in my own family circle.

Throughout my life, there were signs that something was not right in my relationship with my mother. As a child, I always felt guilty and tried to please my mother with whatever she demanded. All she had to do was complain, and I would take over, as long as I had her approval. I actually lived in denial and made excuses for many of her hurtful deeds. I had convinced myself that as her daughter, in her heart, she loved me. Today I feel that it was my father's presence that kept my mother's explosive nature in check. After his death, I had to deal with a different and strange person, which was a great shock to me.

When Oma was more frequently ill, my mother wanted me to take over. She never liked doing housework, and she resented being a caretaker for her sick mother. I tried to reason with her and asked for a compromise. I only stated that she was "asking too much of me." That brought on a hysterical response: "I wish I was dead. I pray every night that I don't commit suicide." She became very defensive and declared her innocence. I was "heartless," "overeducated," and my education "had gone to my head." One time, she even threatened to jump out of our moving car. Dealing with an irrational person made communication an impossible task.

I also had to live with her jealousy. The fact that I had a loving husband who bought me jewelry, which my father never did for my mother, produced great envy of me and my happy marriage. My accomplishment of becoming a teacher at age forty brought no joy to my mother. She too wanted to be a teacher, but Oma would not let her.

I also discovered that my mother was untruthful—in other words, a liar—who enjoyed demonizing me to others, so that they would turn against me. My mother and brother were of the same mind. They bonded against me, while I was pushed to the wayside, which hurt a lot.

Two months after my grandmother died in 1992, my mother visited my son Fred and his wife, Nancy, in Norwalk, Connecticut. This is where my mother told my son that she did not want me from conception, and she had never loved me. Why? She did not want to be tied down with a baby while my father was able to go out on weekends and play in the band. She wanted to have fun too. After I came along, she had to stay home with me, and she did not like it. She never overcame her resentment and anger toward me.

I am certain my grandmother told her daughter, "Don't ever tell that girl you did not want her." But once my grandmother was gone, my mother spoke freely of her feelings toward me to everyone except me. Fred was the only one who informed me of the truth, which I needed to know to come to terms with my relationship to my mother. Yes, the facts were painful, but they helped me in overcoming my guilt. Past experiences made more sense to me too. A very slow, insightful healing process began.

This conflict came to a head when I found out about the slanderous lie my mother told my brother about me. Toni was very angry, accusing me of wanting to cheat him out of his inheritance. It had to do with the money Oma gave my mother. To justify the arrangement with the lawyer, my mother fabricated a completely false story, stating that I "talked her into it." I asked my mother to tell Toni the truth, but she refused.

Tante Anusch from Germany even made a special trip to Chicago to help straighten out this mess, but no one could convince my mother to change her story. What was behind this cover-up? My mother did not want to share the money she had received from her mother with her brother, Jani. Therefore, she denied that the money was from her mother so her brother had no right to claim any of it.

During our confrontations, my mother threatened to hit me. She threw objects at me and made comments such as, "I am sorry that I put you into this world," and "I never want to see you again as long as I live." My husband tried to make peace between my mother and me, but it was hopeless.

The nasty arguments with my mother caused major emotional upheavals in my life. In my mind, I went over and over the hateful things my mother said. I had problems with sleeping, and I knew that my relationship with my mother was at a dead end. My thoughts were so preoccupied while driving one day that I almost collided with a car next to me. My only saving salvations during that time were my husband and prayers.

When my mother invited us to her eightieth birthday party, which she gave for herself, I simply could not go and sit among a family who never spoke a kind word about me. I had realized that, for my own good, I needed to stay away from my mother. I was emotionally drained and despondent.

My mother responded in writing. She wanted me to leave her alone; she wanted to live in peace. My only comfort from her message was that she, not I, cut the ties between us. I was always loyal to my mother and never wanted to forsake her, because I believe in the fourth commandment (honor thy father and mother), and I also wanted a clear conscience.

My mother kept in touch with our son Fred throughout the years. He and his family would visit her every year when they came to Chicago.

On one occasion, my mother approached the subject of "reconciliation." She felt that the younger person has to come to the older person. Fred disagreed with my mother's philosophy and told her so.

However, communication between us was broken. She also had no contact with our son Michael. Nor did my brother reach out to us.

It was in spring of 1997, after I had read an inspiring and insightful article, that I realized the power to fix my relationship with my mother was completely out of my hands. I told my husband that I put my relationship with my mother into God's hands.

This happened later on the same day, after we had done our grocery shopping. It was raining, and to prevent my hair from getting wet, I covered my head with the newspaper I held in my hand. As we were crossing the parking lot, a voice startled me out of my deep thoughts. A man with a huge umbrella was coming toward me. I remember he had gray hair and blue eyes, and he wore a blue sweater. He said to me, "Let me help you. A nice lady like you should not get wet," and he placed the golf umbrella over my head.

I was flustered, and I said, "I'm all right."

But he replied calmly, "I will walk you to your car."

My first impulse was that this had to be a patient from the VA hospital in North Chicago, across the street. The place was home to many patients who suffered from mental disorders. Then I felt embarrassed by the stranger's kind offer. Fritz was walking next to me, pushing the shopping cart. I felt that he too was ill at ease.

The man asked me, "Is this your husband?"

"Yes," I answered.

"You take good care of your husband," he said.

"I will."

I was very uncomfortable and I do not remember any more conversation. The stranger walked me to the passenger side of our car, keeping my head covered with the umbrella.

After I opened the car door, I said, "Thank you very much," and he closed the door after me.

The stranger's kind deed just overwhelmed me, and I covered my face and cried. I never looked up or turned my head, for my heartache was too great.

Fritz told me that when he was in the car, he looked where the man was going, but he had disappeared. He no longer was in the parking lot.

It was peculiar that the man selected me because there were many people walking around. The stranger's simple act of kindness touched my heart, because my own mother would not do this for me. I also remembered that only a few hours ago, I had declared out loud my surrender to God by placing my relationship with my mother into his hands. When Fritz said that the man had disappeared, I concluded that he must have been a messenger from God. He comforted me, and I realized he wanted me to look after my husband. That was my first responsibility, and I should not worry about my mother. Six months later my husband was diagnosed with metastasized prostate cancer. The meeting with the stranger was a prediction of what was to come. Every time I think of this meeting, I feel comforted.

In October 1997, Fritz needed major orthopedic surgery, where they removed eighteen centimeters of cancerous bone. He was hospitalized and in rehab for many weeks. He recovered completely. During his illness, I kept praying to God to grant us another ten years together. Yes, this prayer was fulfilled. Fritz lived another ten years and eight months. God was gracious to us and blessed us.

I tried to be helpful too, studying about supplements and herbal remedies. I had my husband's full trust and confidence, and he was willing to go along to promote his well being. Fritz made an amazing recovery from this surgery.

How did we survive the tumultuous years with my mother? We visited our son Fred and his family each year and traveled to various destinations across the United States. On one European trip with my cousins Chris and Grace Marx, we saw the Passion Play in Oberammergau, Germany, and visited Austria and Switzerland. Another trip involved a grand tour of Germany, where we met and became dear friends with Marlin and Karen Reeck from Appleton, Wisconsin. We also loved Hawaii and made several trips to the islands. But as the last six years of my husband's life became filled with more surgeries and illnesses, we were homebound.

I also kept physically active throughout the years. In Lindenhurst, I went for long bike rides during the summer and took exercise classes in winter. When we moved to Trevor, I joined Jazzercise class in 1999, and I still attend four to five sessions per week, at age seventy-five. I feel blessed to be able to participate in the Jazzercise workouts.

On December 2, 2005, my mother died. As expected, my brother never called me. He contacted my son Fred and gave him the funeral information. The news of my mother's death made me nervous and upset. I ordered a large bouquet of white flowers. I chose the color white because it represents purity and innocence. That is how I felt about my birth—it was not of my choosing. I also ordered a ribbon with only one word on it: "Mother."

Michael, Mary, Fritz, and I arrived at the funeral home early, before anyone else was there. I needed to see my mother; I wanted closure with this part of my life. I cried for all the heartaches and pain that could have been avoided if there had been some "love." What a wasted life of deception and hatred!

When I looked at my flowers that stood to the side of the casket, I could not believe what I saw. The bouquet, which I had spent a lot of money on, was all wilted, and there was no ribbon. Michael called the flower shop and complained. They brought a ribbon marked "Mother," but the man denied any knowledge of the wilted flowers. When he brought them they were fresh, he said, but these flowers were no longer his responsibility.

The sad-looking flowers made me very unhappy. I actually felt ashamed, because the people coming to my mother's wake were aware of our family situation, and now I was represented by this pathetic-looking bouquet.

The thought occurred to me much later. I told my husband that these wilted flowers actually represented my relationship with my mother, and he agreed. Was it a sign from God? We were unable to come up with a different explanation.

When my brother, Toni, and family arrived, I asked to speak to him privately. He agreed. I listened patiently to all his complaints against me, beginning with my treatment of him in Wolkersdorf, how I was the favored one in the family, and so on. He also defended our mother, saying I provoked her and picked fights with her, and she had no other choice. I knew the closed-mindedness of my brother, and it was useless to reason with him or try to defend myself.

I did ask him, though, if he was willing to forgive me for hitting him in Wolkersdorf. He answered yes. The next day, he told Fred, "Your mother asked for forgiveness, but it is too late for that."

I asked Toni for a copy of my mother's will and the return of all my family pictures in her house. Sure, he promised. Considering how unreliable my brother had been in the past, I asked him three times for these items, which annoyed him. The next day he told Fred, "I am not sending your mother a copy of the will. It will be in the newspaper anyway." I did get two packages with my family pictures, but no copy of the will.

We left before other people came to the wake. Throughout this upsetting ordeal, I remained calm, possessing a strength that surprised me. Normally I would have been a nervous, stammering individual, but not this time. I was completely at ease. I told my husband that someone had given me the strength that I did not possess on my own.

Due to a flight delay, Fred and Nancy could not attend the wake, but they were present for the funeral the next day. My brother informed Fred that he was in my mother's last will, because Toni insisted that my share of my inheritance should go to him. My son sent me a copy of my mother's will, which stated, "I have intentionally not provided for my daughter Elizabeth M. Wilms, and my grandson Michael A. Wilms, in this will." Even though I expected the disinheritance from my mother, the rejection still hurt. But Michael? What had he done to her to receive this treatment?

Fred and Nancy felt that I did not deserve my mother's rejection, and they agreed to divide their inheritance with Michael and me. I was very grateful for my son's generosity and sense of fairness. Compared to the total value of my parents' estate, my son's inheritance was a modest amount.

In May 2006, Fred and Nancy separated, and their divorce was granted in November 2007.

In April 2008, my husband was diagnosed with bladder cancer. We were both devastated by the bad news. Surgery was recommended by the doctor. I witnessed the decline of Fritz's strength, and I did not favor surgery. Fritz, however, felt that he had no other choice.

It so happened that on Fritz's birthday, August 4, 2008, he had surgery at Evanston Hospital in Evanston, Illinois. On the same day, our son Fred, along with Mina and Peter, left for China for the Olympics, and Michael started a new job with the US Postal Service.

Surgery went well, but Fritz was moved to the Intensive Care Unit. I spent the night at my friend Wilma Stafflinger's house in Morton Grove. We were sitting in the front room, reminiscing about the past, when for no reason at all, I stopped and asked Wilma about the time. She said, "It is about 10:20 p.m. Let's go to bed at 10:30."

It turned out that was the exact moment Fritz's heart stopped. I feel Fritz's spirit sought me out at that instant. Wilma and I agreed, and we developed goose bumps. The doctor felt that one organ shut down, and a chain reaction followed in Fritz's body. Even though Fritz was revived, he was in a coma and the prognosis was not very good.

Holding his hand, I talked to my husband, telling him I loved him and wanted him to come back. His response was immediate: he moved his left leg and his knee jerked upward.

"It was an automatic reflex," the doctor claimed.

Another time, I stroked his forehead and said, "Fritz, it's me, Elizabeth, remember me? You and I have been married for almost fifty years." Instantly, a tear appeared on the inside of his left eye, where I was standing. His other eye was blocked from my view due to all the tubes in his face. Again, I informed the doctor.

"He is full of fluids," he said.

While the doctor may have had valid reasons for his explanations, I truly believe my husband heard me and his spirit responded.

Fritz's condition continued to deteriorate. He needed more blood transfusions, more oxygen, and kidney dialysis. I was approached to give permission to turn off the machines. This was a very difficult decision for me, even though Fritz had given me the authority. On

August 9, 2008, five days later, the machines were turned off, and within fewer than five minutes, Fritz was gone. Michael and Mary were with me to comfort me, but I was devastated by the loss of my dear husband.

We waited for the return of Fred, Mina, and Peter from China. On August 19, 2008, Fritz was buried at the Veterans Cemetery in Union Grove, Wisconsin.

Of course I had a lot of support from my sons, my grandchildren, my friends, our pastors, and the church congregation. But the house was so empty, and I missed Fritz. My depressing thoughts gave me tension headaches and butterflies in my stomach. I realized these symptoms could actually make me physically sick, and I knew I had to occupy myself with different things and ideas.

Our church offered a Grief Share program, which I attended with six to eight other people who had lost loved ones. I found the sessions very beneficial.

I donated Fritz's well-kept US Air Force uniform to the Lakes Region Historical Society in Antioch, Illinois. It is on display with several nice pictures of Fritz for future generations to view.

Ladies from our church, including me, helped out with triplets who were born to the Taylor family, from our congregation. While the triplets were sleeping, Linda Rullman, who babysat with me, encouraged me to tell her about my past, and she told me many times, "You have to write a book."

For the last two years, I have been teaching in our church's Lutheran Girls Pioneer Program. We meet once a week in the evenings and learn about leadership, citizenship, first aid, cooking, and nature. This is something I enjoy doing. I also belong to our Older Wisconsin Lutheran Synod (OWLS), which offers monthly activities, like plays, ballgames, dinners out, etc. Besides that, I attend two weekly Bible studies classes.

I visit my son Fred and grandchildren Mina and Peter in Norwalk, Connecticut, every year. I see my son Michael and Mary, frequently, since they live close by. For the past year, I have been working on my life story. It has been a time-consuming project, but I needed to open up and write it.

I do not know why the Lord gave me the mother I had. Maybe one day I will get an answer. In the meantime, I try not to dwell on the hurtful past. I look forward to every new day that is given to me, and I try not to repeat the mistakes that were made.

I have forgiven my mother, my brother, and the communist partisans. I harbor no resentment and bitterness against them or anyone. Forgiveness is a gift I gave to myself. It freed me from the past and helped me move on with my life. The elimination of bitterness and resentment gave me peace within my heart. At the same time, doing away with negative feelings has also improved my psychological and physical well being.

I found more comfort in reading Rick Warren's book *The Purpose Driven Life,* where he states, "You are not an accident."

Though there may be unplanned pregnancies, there are no unwanted children. God has lovingly planned each life with a larger purpose in mind. There is a reason I survived World War II, when so many thousands or maybe even millions did not. There is a reason I waged my own inner war long after World War II was over, and there is a reason I decided to write and publish this book.

May my story encourage, comfort, and inspire other struggling individuals who are presently waging their own private battles.

About the Author

It was not until the 1990s that my experiences were brought into the foreground again.

During this time, the former Yugoslavia was falling apart, and the Serbian majority committed all kinds of brutalities against the minorities. This news motivated me to write down my experiences, since I had been one of their victims many years ago, after World War II.

I was separated from my father for close to eight years. I was apart from my mother for three years. My two-year-old brother and I were placed in several liquidation camps in Yugoslavia. What saved us were the aid packages from our relatives in Chicago.

But hidden among this public turmoil was a dark family secret.

Presently I am a retired teacher and a widow living in Trevor, Wisconsin. I have two grown sons and two grandchildren. Much of my time is spent doing volunteer work in our church and school. I also attend several Bible classes. This is my first book.

Bibliography

Danube Swabian Association of the USA. *Genocide of the Ethnic Germans in Yugoslavia 1944-1948*. Chicago: Award Printing Corp, 2001.

de Zayas, Alfred. *A Terrible Revenge*, 2nd ed. New York, St. Martin's Press, 1994.

de Zayas, Alfred. *Nemesis at Potsdam*: *The Expulsions of the Germans*. Rockport: Picton Press, 1998.

Douglas, R. M. *Orderly and Humane: The Expulsion of the Germans after the Second World War*. New Haven: Yale University Press, 2012.

Fergusen, Wallace K. and Geoffrey Bruun. *A Survey of European Civilization*. Boston: Houghton Mifflin Company, 1969.

Hess, Nikolaus and Michael Gross. *Heimatbuch der Banater Schwestergemeinden St. Hubert Charleville Soltur*. Muenchen: Selbstverlag, 1981.

Koehler Eckert, Eve. *Seven Susannahs: Daughters of the Danube*. Cedarburg: Graphic Inc., 1976.

Kuechel, Anna. *Jugend im Banat*. Personal correspondence. Translated by Elizabeth M. Wilms, 1992.

Metaxas, Eric. *Bonhoeffer: Pastor, Martyr, Prophet, Spy. A Righteous Gentile versus the Third Reich*. Nashville: Thomas Nelson, 2010.

Seamands, David A. *Healing for Damaged Emotions: Recovering from Memories That Cause Our Pain*. Colorado Springs: Victor Books, 1991.

Springenschmid, Karl. *Our Lost Children: Janissaries?* Translated by John Adam Koehler and Eve Eckert Koehler. Milwaukee: Bolk Printing Company, 1980.

Stenger Frey, Katherine. *The Danube Swabians: A People with Portable Roots.* Belleville, Ontario: Mika Publishing Company, 1982.

Walter, Elizabeth B. *Barefoot in the Rubble.* Palatine: Pannonia Press, 1997.

Warren, Rick. *The Purpose-Driven Life.* Grand Rapids: Zondervan, 2002.

Endnotes

At my request, and for readers of these memoirs who may wish to read other survivors' stories, Eve Koehler has compiled a list of authors who "speak for the silent," compelled to share their experiences with Americans who have no idea this genocide occurred.

The memoirs below are listed in chronological order of publication.

Wlossak Muller, Traudie (1982). *The Whip: My Homecoming.* Red Hill, Australia: Golden Leaf Publishers. Traudie tells of her fight to stay alive during three years in the infamous Mitrovica Camp. (Available through university inter-library loan.)

Tenz Horwath, Maria (1989). *The Innocent Must Pay.* Translated by John A. Koehler. Munich: Eugen Verlag. The story of a teenage girl in a Yugoslavian starvation camp. English edition: University of Mary, Bismarck, ND.

Walter, Elizabeth B. *Barefoot in the Rubble* (1997). Foreword by Prof. Charles Barber. Northeastern Illinois University. Palatine, IL: Pannonia Press. Barber writes, "Those of us who have read her story are in her debt."

Owen Lang, Luisa (2003). *Casualty of War: A Childhood Remembered.* Foreword by Prof. C. Barber. College Station: Texas A & M University Press. The author is a professor emeritus of art education, Wright State University, Ohio.

Flotz Hoeger, Katherine (2004). *A Pebble in My Shoe: A Memoir.* Palatine, IL: Pannonia Press. Katherine quotes a passage that all these authors believed in during their years of freedom: "Do not forget the things your eyes have seen, or let them slip from your heart; in your lifetime, teach them to your children" (Deuteronomy 4:9).

For a complete bibliography, see www.molidorf.com.

Made in the USA
Lexington, KY
14 November 2013